T0253857

Project Management for Practice

Daud Alam · Uwe Gühl

Project Management for Practice

A Guide and Toolbox for Successful Projects

 Springer

Daud Alam
EDV-Beratung Alam
Sindelfingen, Germany

Uwe Gühl
Stuttgart, Germany

ISBN 978-3-662-65161-2   ISBN 978-3-662-65159-9   (eBook)
https://doi.org/10.1007/978-3-662-65159-9

© Springer-Verlag GmbH Germany, part of Springer Nature 2022
This work is subject to copyright. All rights are reserved by the Publisher, whether the whole or part of the material is concerned, specifically the rights of translation, reprinting, reuse of illustrations, recitation, broadcasting, reproduction on microfilms or in any other physical way, and transmission or information storage and retrieval, electronic adaptation, computer software, or by similar or dissimilar methodology now known or hereafter developed.
The use of general descriptive names, registered names, trademarks, service marks, etc. in this publication does not imply, even in the absence of a specific statement, that such names are exempt from the relevant protective laws and regulations and therefore free for general use.
The publisher, the authors, and the editors are safe to assume that the advice and information in this book are believed to be true and accurate at the date of publication. Neither the publisher nor the authors or the editors give a warranty, expressed or implied, with respect to the material contained herein or for any errors or omissions that may have been made. The publisher remains neutral with regard to jurisdictional claims in published maps and institutional affiliations.

Responsible Editor: Petra Steinmueller
This Springer imprint is published by the registered company Springer-Verlag GmbH, DE, part of Springer Nature.
The registered company address is: Heidelberger Platz 3, 14197 Berlin, Germany

This book is dedicated to Nafisa Alam, Micha A.,
our families and our friendship.

شد آموزگاری از آن پیشه ام

که بهبود خلق است اندیشه ام

سعدی

Foreword

This is an excellent book for everyone who wants to find out more about project management.

Written using the authors' wide-ranging experiences solving real-life problems and their many years training students and lecturing, this book is a well-structured approach, complete with practical steps to facilitate all project management tasks. Each chapter starts with a set of learning objectives and ends with a summary of the relevant findings. In between, you find descriptions of sample problems taken from the automotive and IT sectors as well as content illustrating typical project phases, advice on strategies, practice examples, document templates, and checklists to work through and many well-illustrated solutions and practical tips.

As well as providing an introductory theory on project management, the book also offers the tools readers need to bring their own projects to a successful conclusion. Although an introductory text, more experienced project management practitioners can also benefit from the interesting content, templates, and checklists which will help them to implement their project practices in even more successful ways.

The second edition is even more valuable by considering agile aspects and change management. Additional tasks help to achieve a better understanding.

I highly recommend this interesting and neatly constructed book to all beginners who are looking for their first introductory book on project management.

June 2020

Arnon Rungsawang
Associate Prof. in Computer Engineering
Kasetsart University
Bangkok, Thailand

Project management is nothing new. Someone might even come up with the idea of asking whether the world needs another book on project management. In my opinion, the answer is: Yes, however.

Due to the constantly increasing competition and the simultaneously shorter and shorter product cycles, projects in the economy have been changing significantly for some time. The resources (time, money and capacity) available are being reduced even further, the project participants and stakeholders are distributed across different regions of the world and the desired goal is to be achieved as safely as never before.

For this reason, it is even more important than ever to know exactly what the result of the project should be and how to measure it. There is a need for a clear structure in project phases as well as the definition of milestones by which the project and its progress can be monitored. The monitoring, often referred to as controlling, must keep the really relevant aspects in mind. However, the effort for controlling and the associated reporting to budget responsible persons or customers must not exceed that of the professional project processing. Efficiency is one reason for this, the motivation of the processors the other, almost even more important one.

The goal-oriented monitoring of project progress sometimes leads to the realization that the chosen path was not quite optimal. Further action, possibly even milestones that have been set, must at least be called into question, often needing to be completely redefined. Therefore, an open approach to failures or mistakes is a key factor for the success of a project. Acknowledging this situation allows for steps to be taken to analyze the cause and replan the project.

Project management today not only requires the ability to always flexibly adapt the project to current conditions, but much more has to be taken into account for successful goal achievement and all of this has to be done in a shorter time.

This book has structured the topic of project management well and thus made it practice-oriented. It offers the project manager a flexible support to successfully meet the ever-increasing demands.

June 2020

Dr. Gritt Ahrens
Director of Quality Management
Daimler Buses
Neu-Ulm

Preface

Every day we have projects to do in our professional and private lives. Our work includes not only project management but also the transfer of the corresponding knowledge. This took place at various project management training courses and lectures, e.g. at the Stuttgart Chamber of Industry and Commerce, Hochschule Pforzheim, Hochschule Albstadt-Sigmaringen and at Kasetsart University in Bangkok and Sriracha, Thailand. Here, both on the part of the participants and on our part as lecturers, there was a demand for a book with a practical reference that could serve as a toolbox for project management.

The aim of this book is not only to introduce the topic theoretically, but also to give the reader the necessary tools for use in practice. The most important terms and phases of project management are explained in compliance with standards. Subsequently, this book deals with cross-project cross-cutting issues and specific content with regard to the project phases. Agile aspects are considered in a separate chapter. Tips and hints, examples, templates and checklists as well as tasks and solutions from project practice in the automotive and IT sector supplement the content. This should give you a good and quick access to the topic of project management and help you to successfully complete your project. This book is designed for the following target groups:

- Curious people who want to acquire first knowledge about and understanding of the topic of project management.
- Students (Bachelor and Master).
- Participants in a project management training who are looking for training materials.
- Project management interested people who want to prepare themselves optimally for their first project.

- Project management experts who want to learn additional aspects as well as templates and checklists for even more successful projects.

The following offers you this book:

- Practical relevance
- This book combines many years of experience in projects with the relevant theories of project management. This should make it easier for you to implement what you have learned theoretically in practice. In addition to extensive explanations of the relevant topics of project management, you will receive practical support in the form of examples, templates and checklists.
- Method examples
- This book describes methods that you can use in the different phases, depending on the conditions in your project.
- Goals and results
- The beginning of a chapter lists the specific learning objectives. At the end of a chapter, corresponding findings are summarized.
- Tasks and solutions
- Practice exercises can be used to test the understanding of the content of a chapter.
- Templates

We would like to thank our families first and foremost, who made this book possible with their support. For the great help in reviewing the automatically generated translation we would like to thank Terry Lyons, adjunct professor of the Queensland University of Technology, Australia, very much. He significantly improved the quality of this book and made sure that the content can be conveyed better. We would especially like to thank Prof. Dr. Christian Kücherer for his very intensive involvement with this work and his excellent suggestions and explanations. Thank you very much for your support, your review and constructive criticism to Nadia Alam (IT Rollout Manager, Strategic project and schedule management R&D, Mercedes-Benz AG, Germany), Diana Alam (Head of office, IHK Reutlingen, Germany), Marina Alam (Production Engineer, Master's degree, Friedrich-Alexander-University of Erlangen, Germany), Pia von Berlepsch (Manager Product Development, Miles & More GmbH), Arno Bohnet, Martin Börger (entrusted with tasks relating to cyber and IT security and administrative digitization at the Hessian Ministry of the Interior), Martin Carr, Murat Ercan (Senior Project Manager, Architecture & Construction Management, Hugo Boss AG), Klaus Franz (Quality Assurance Manager, dictaJetQC GmbH, Wiesbaden), Doris Helzle, Frank Jörder (Director GJC Gnädinger und Jörder Consulting GmbH), Prof. Dr.-Ing. Guido Kramann (Brandenburg University of Applied Sciences, Germany), Nicole Merkel-Hilf, Dagmar Michels, Ebba Rauch, Dr. Sophie L. Otterbach (University of Hohenheim, Germany) and Sabine Willmann.

Stuttgart Sindelfingen   Daud Alam
August 2020   Uwe Gühl

Contents

About the Authors

Daud Alam Economist, born in 1955 in Herat, Afghanistan, began his career for a Siemens subsidiary. The second stage of his career was the software company Wesser Informatik. He then worked for the Project Management Academy in Stuttgart as a project manager. Most recently, he worked for Mercedes-Benz AG for almost 20 years. He taught the first edition of the book for five semesters at the Albstadt-Sigmaringen University of Applied Sciences. Currently, he conducts seminars in Germany and abroad for AKKA Technologies SE and the Daimler Education Academy. He gives lectures to Mercedes-Benz AG students at the DHBW Stuttgart and at the Pforzheim University of Applied Sciences.

Uwe Gühl Dr.-Ing. Dipl. Inform., born in 1966 in Offenbach/Main, Germany, works freelance in the areas of IT project management of international on-/off-shore projects, IT quality and software test management as well as moderation and international team development. After training and working in the field of social security, he studied computer science and received a doctorate in mechanical engineering. He researched and worked in companies in the automotive, banking, trade, logistics and media industries as well as at universities both in Germany and internationally in Switzerland, France, U.S.A., India and Thailand.

List of Figures

List of Tables

Introduction

1

Project management is playing an increasingly important role in today's professional world. For example, the project management activities of an engineer during a typical workday have increased significantly from about 9% to over 16% in recent years [7, p. 27]. The Deutsche-Bank study "Projektwirtschaft 2020" predicts that the share of projects in the value creation within the entire German economy will increase from 2% in 2007 to 15% in 2020 [12]. According to an analysis by the Project Management Institute (PMI), the global demand for project management experts is growing: by 2027, about 87.7 million will be needed [17].

In order to be able to talk about project management, a common understanding of the underlying terminology is necessary. Terms can only be used correctly if they are understood correctly.

1.1 Definitions

For the topic of project management, there are somewhat different definitions of different professional organizations and committees such as the German Institute for Standardization (DIN) [6], the German Association for Project Management (GPM) [10] and the Project Management Institute [18]. Companies also partly define their own standards in project management with individual structuring and naming of the project phases. The terms have been checked, brought together for easy understanding and defined and explained in the corresponding context in accordance with the standards.

A common (technical) language is also necessary for projects, so every project should have a glossary. Further explanations can be found in Sect. 2.4.4. The glossary of this book can be found on page 201. First, the fundamental question arises: What is a project?

© Springer-Verlag GmbH Germany, part of Springer Nature 2022
D. Alam and U. Gühl, *Project Management for Practice*,
https://doi.org/10.1007/978-3-662-65159-9_1

Project

According to DIN 69901-5, a project is an "intent that is essentially characterized by the uniqueness of the conditions in their entirety". A project is characterized by a target specification with temporal, financial and personnel limitations [6]. It is typically new and unique, complex and requires a project-specific organization. Characteristics of a project are:

- Defined goal
  The result can be, for example, a product, a system or a process.
- Uniqueness
  Typically, it is something new.
- Temporal limitation
  There is a beginning and an end.
- Resource limitation
- Sufficient complexity
- Cross-sectoral
  This is generally the case in large organizations.

So a project is not about the execution of standard tasks. For example, the maintenance of software is an ongoing task. But if, for example, releases are delivered at certain times, each release can be considered a project with release planning, preparation and implementation. Management is understood to mean the "management of socio-technical systems in terms of people and things using professional methods. In the dimension of things related to management, it is about coping with the tasks that arise from the highest goals of the system in the dimension of people related to management, it is about the right way to deal with all the people on whose cooperation the management is dependent for the task to be carried out" [25].

Next is the fundamental question of this book: What is project management?

Project Management

DIN 69901-5 defines project management as "the totality of leadership tasks, organisation, techniques and means for the initiation, definition, planning, control and completion of projects" [6].

Project management therefore includes the coordination of people and the optimal use of resources to achieve project goals.

There are also further specifications for the term "project management". The Project Management Institute explains that "Project Management is the application of knowledge, skills, tools, and techniques to project activities to meet project requirements" [19].

The Society for Informatics understands project management to mean "leading, coordinating, controlling and monitoring the project".

Dr. Martin Barnes, President of the British Association for Project Management (APM) from 2003 to 2012, summed up: "At its most fundamental, project management is about people getting things done" [1].

1.2 Successful Projects

Studies confirm that many IT projects fail and many more projects exceed deadlines and/ or costs. As can be seen in Fig. 1.1, the percentage of successful projects according to the Standish Group increased continuously from 1994 to 2012. It should be noted that in 2015, the Standish Group redefined the term "successful" [11]. The background is that if a project has "reached its goal", this does not necessarily reflect the corresponding customer value. The Standish Group has found that projects have kept to time and cost and achieved their goal, but the customer was not satisfied. So in the new definition of the term "successful" the customer benefit was taken into account, which led to a reduction in the proportion of successfully completed projects by seven percentage points [26].

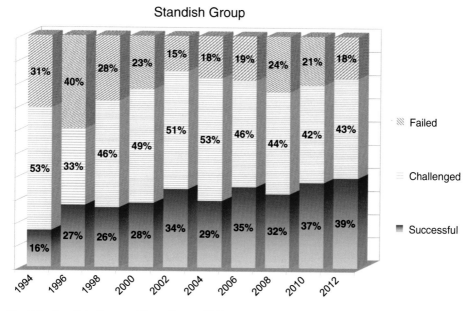

Fig. 1.1 Standish Group – Chaos Report 2013

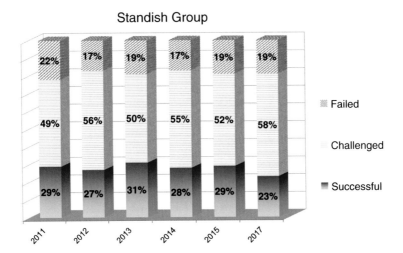

Fig. 1.2 Standish Group – Overview with updated definition of "successful"

The situation in 2017 is as follows according to Fig. 1.2 [24]:

- Failed = Failed:
  According to the report, in 2017 around 19% of the projects started were complete failures.
- Challenged = Time and cost overrun:
  In 2017, according to the Chaos Report, 58% of the projects at least partially did not meet the wishes and requirements of the client.
- Successful = Successfully completed:
  23% of the projects considered in 2017 were completed on time and within budget and achieved the goal.

Every project manager wants to successfully complete projects. So why are projects successful and why do projects fail? The most common reasons for failed projects are [9]:

1. poor communication,
2. unclear requirements and goals,
3. politics, departmental egoism or internal competence disputes.

The main reasons for failed software projects are, according to an international study among developers (multiple responses possible) [4]
1. changing or poorly documented requirements (48%);
2. underfunding (40%);
3. a poor team or poor organizational leadership (37%).

Success factors in project management are listed in Table 1.1 [23].

Table 1.1 Success factors in project management

No.	Success factor	Percent (%)	Refer to, see
1.	Involving users	15.9	Sect. 2.3
2.	Support by top management	13.9	Sect. 3.1.3, Fig. 2.8
3.	Clear requirements	13.0	Sects. 2.1, 2.4
4.	Reasonable planning	9.6	Sect. 3.2
5.	Realistic Expectations	8.2	Sects. 2.3, 3.1.6, 3.2.8
6.	Small Project Milestones	7.7	Sects. 3.2.4, 3.3.3
7.	Competent employees	7.2	Sects. 2.3, 3.2.6
8.	Clear responsibility (ownership)	5.3	Sects. 3.1.3, 3.1.6, 3.2.6
9.	Clear visions and themes	2.9	Sects. 3.1.4, 3.1.6
10.	Hardworking, goal-oriented project team	2.4	Sect. 2.3
	Other success factors	13.9	

Projects nowadays are characterized by a focus on defined target groups, increasing complexity and growing expectations, for example with regard to mobile communication and required cost efficiency. A challenge is the increasing international cooperation with onshore, offshore and nearshore parts,[1] increased environmental requirements and increased cost and time pressure.

This book is intended to help you ensure that your projects can be counted among the successful ones. Table 1.1 contains references to sections in this book which explain the mentioned success factors in more detail.

1.3 Project Management Process Models

In project management, procedure models have been developed and standards defined by different parties. The following is a selection:

- International standards
  - Guide to the Project Management Body of Knowledge (PMBOK-Guide) [16]
    The PMBOK® is the standard and central reference of the US-based Project Management Institute [18]. This is one of the leading project management standards in the world, along with the ICB and PRINCE2 (see below).
  - IPMA Competence Baseline (ICB)

---

[1] onshore = outsourcing within the country of origin, offshore = outsourcing abroad, nearshore = outsourcing to a neighboring country (like Mexico for the USA, and the Eastern part of Europe for European countries).

The International Project Management Association (IPMA) with headquarters in the Netherlands has more than 70 national member associations, with the GPM Deutsche Gesellschaft für Projektmanagement e. V. (GPM) being the German representative. IPMA develops and promotes project management and has defined an international project management standard with the ICB [13].

– PRINCE2
Originally, PRINCE[2] was the British government's standard for managing projects in information technology (IT). The further development PRINCE2 is the de-facto standard for project management in Great Britain, but is also widespread in more than 50 other countries [2]. PRINCE2 provides a project framework that is constantly being developed as a best practice approach.

- National Standards
  – German National Competence Baseline (NCB) [27]
  The German translation of the ICB (see above) published in 2017 in version 4.0 is considered the IPMA's NCB and is the GPM's central reference.
  – DIN 69900 [5], DIN 69901-5 [6]
  The project management standards DIN 69900 and DIN 69901 cover basics, descriptions and terms from the fields of project management and network planning.
  – V-Modell XT [3]
  The V-Modell XT is a project management standard for developing IT systems that is mandatory in the public sector in Germany. It covers the areas of project management, quality assurance, configuration management, system development and specifications for the tendering and awarding of projects.
- Company-specific standards
  In particular, larger companies define company-specific project management approaches based on standards. This is to ensure that projects in companies define uniform committees, use the same procedures, report in a standardized manner, and can be efficiently supported by templates and instructions. Examples are:
  – ITPM at BMW Group [15]
  – Houston at Daimler AG [8]
  – Project Management Excellence at Siemens AG [22]
- Standards in special areas
  In information technology there are several process models defined for software development like:
  – Waterfall model [20]
  This is a sequential model that is often used in software development. Typical phases are analysis, design, implementation, testing and maintenance. Output values of a phase are input values for the subsequent phase.

---

[2] PRINCE stands for "**Pr**ojects **in** **C**ontrolled **E**nvironments"

- V-Model [3]

  This is a project management method for development projects that originally comes from IT. In this case, the waterfall model is extended by test stages, with each development phase corresponding to test phases.

- Rational Unified Process (RUP) [14]

  RUP includes a software development process on the one hand and corresponding tools from IBM on the other. It provides for iterations and defines the following four phases:

  Inception

  Elaboration

  Construction

  Transition

- Scrum [21]

  Scrum is understood as a framework in the field of project management. It is a simple process model with few rules and is based on agile software development. Section 4.2 introduces Scrum in detail.

  These standards are intended to ensure that projects are carried out with the same procedure and with the same documentation in a certain quality standard. However, it should be noted that projects are very different in terms of goals, size, time frame and scope. With tailoring, project-specific adaptations of the process models are made. This is intended to ensure that the process models can be used for all project variants.

However, practice shows that the defined standards are not always 100% implementable. For example, in international cooperation projects there are different process models of the participating partners, so that only one process model can be used or a compromise must be found.

Based on the project experiences of the authors, cross-sectional topics are described in this book. In addition, project phases in classical projects are presented as well as aspects of agile projects. The developed content is compared with actual process models.

1.4 Structure of the Book

Chapter 2 explains general topics of the project work. Cross-sectional topics such as requirements, change management, project culture, communication, documentation, quality, risk management and methods are project phase-spanning. They apply throughout the project and are not attributable only to individual project phases. As an example, project culture plays an important role throughout the project duration in both classical and agile projects. Chapter 3 focuses on the individual project phases in classical projects, starting with the strategy phase, through the planning and implementation phases to the closure phase. Chapter 4 explains agility in projects. Chapter 5 rounds off the book with an outlook. In addition, you will find in Chap. 6 templates that you can use as aids in your projects.

1.5   Summary

Project management is becoming increasingly important in   professional life. Even today, a large proportion of projects fail, so it makes sense to deal with the topic of project management in more detail. A project is unique, time-limited, usually complex and equipped with limited resources.

Project management means the planning and implementation of a project. The terms project and project management are defined differently. National and international organizations set project management standards such as the PMBOK Guide or the IPMA Competence Baseline. In addition, there are also company-specific processes and procedures as well as for special areas.

1.6   Problems

1.1 Motivation Why should one deal with the topic of project management?

1.2 Project Definition
(a) What is a project?
(b) What are the characteristics of a project?

1.3 Project Management How is project management defined?

1.4 Success Factors Name at least three success factors for projects.

1.5 Failure What are the most common reasons for project failure?

References

1. Association for project management (apm): What is project management? (2020). https://www.apm.org.uk/resources/what-is-project-management/. Accessed: 23 Aug 2022
2. Axelos: What is prince2®? (2020). https://www.axelos.com/best-practice-solutions/prince2/what-is-prince2?. Accessed: 23 Aug 2022
3. Der Beauftragte der Bundesregierung für Informationstechnik: V-Modell XT (2018). https://www.cio.bund.de/Web/DE/Architekturen-und-Standards/V-Modell-XT/vmodell_xt_node.html. Accessed: 23. Aug. 2022
4. Developers Alliance: Developer insights report (2015). https://www.developersalliance.org/developer-insights-report-2015. Accessed: 23 Aug 2022

5. DIN Deutsches Institut für Normung e. V.: DIN 69900:2009-01, Projektmanagement – Netzplantechnik; Beschreibungen und Begriffe (2009). https://www.beuth.de/en/standard/din-69900/113428266. Accessed: 23 Aug 2022
6. DIN Deutsches Institut für Normung e. V.: DIN 69901-5:2009-01, Projektmanagement – Projektmanagementsysteme – Teil 5: Begriffe (2009). https://www.beuth.de/en/standard/din-69901-5/113428752. Accessed: 23 Aug 2022
7. Eigner, M., Stelzer, R.: Ein Leitfaden für Product Development und Life Cycle Management. Springer-Verlag Berlin-Heidelberg (2009)
8. Gorriz, M.: IT-Prozesse erfolgreich standardisieren. Vortrag automotiveDay Cebit 2010 (2010)
9. GPM Deutsche Gesellschaft für Projektmanagement e. V.: Ergebnisse der Projektmanagement Studie 2008 – Erfolg und Scheitern im Projektmanagement – Gemeinsame Studie der GPM Deutsche Gesellschaft für Projektmanagement e. V. und PA Consulting Group (2008). https://www.gpm-ipma.de/know_how/studienergebnisse/pm_studie_2008_erfolg_und_scheitern_im_pm.html. Accessed: 23 Aug 2022
10. GPM Deutsche Gesellschaft für Projektmanagement e. V.: Homepage (2022). https://www.gpm-ipma.de. Accessed: 23 Aug 2022
11. Hastie, S., Wojewoda, S.: Standish Group 2015 Chaos Report – Q&A with Jennifer Lynch on Oct 04, 2015 (2015). https://www.infoq.com/articles/standish-chaos-2015/. Accessed: 23 Aug 2022
12. Hirschbiegel, K.E.: Die Trends im Projektmanagement – ein Überblick (2020). https://www.tecchannel.de/a/die-trends-im-projektmanagement-ein-ueberblick,2064194. Accessed: 23 Aug 2022
13. Home – IPMA International Project Management Association: Homepage (2022). https://www.ipma.world/. Accesses: 23 Aug 2022
14. Jacobson, I., Booch, G., Rumbaugh, J.: The unified software development process. Addison Wesley (1999)
15. Priemuth, T.: Überblick und Grundlagen IT- Qualitätsmanagement der BMW Group (2006). http://bis.informatik.uni-leipzig.de/de/Lehre/0506/SS/SQMmore/files?get=vortragpriemuthbmwgroup.pdf. Accessed: 23 Aug 2022
16. Project Management Institute: A Guide to the Project Management Body of Knowledge (PMBOK Guide 6), 6th ed. Project Management Institute (2017)
17. Project Management Institute: Project Management, Job Growth and Talent Gap, 2017–2027 (2017). https://www.pmi.org/-/media/pmi/documents/public/pdf/learning/job-growth-report.pdf. Accessed: 1 Aug 2020
18. Project Management Institute: Homepage (2020). https://www.pmi.org/. Accessed: 23 Aug 2022
19. Project Management Institute: What is project management? (2020). https://www.pmi.org/about/learn-about-pmi/what-is-project-management. Accessed: 23 Aug 2022
20. Royce, W.W.: Managing the development of large software systems. In: Proceedings IEEE WESCON, 26. Auflage, pp. 328–338. Institute of Electrical and Electronics Engineers (1970). https://leadinganswers.typepad.com/leading_answers/files/original_waterfall_paper_winston_royce.pdf. Accessed: 23 Aug 2022
21. Schwaber, K., Sutherland, J.: The Scrum Guide (2020). https://www.scrumguides.org/scrumguide.html. Accessed: 23 Aug 2022
22. Siemens A.,G.: Corporate Technology Office Project-Management: Project management for practice (2011)
23. The Standish Group: The Standish Group Report – Chaos (2009). https://www.projectsmart.co.uk/white-papers/chaos-report.pdf. Accessed: 23 Aug 2022
24. The Standish Group: Project Resolution Benchmark Demo Report (2018). https://www.standish-group.com/sample_research/. Accessed: 23 Aug 2022

25. Ulrich, P., Fluri, E.: Management. Eine konzentrierte Einführung. UTB Haupt, Bern Stuttgart (1988)
26. Weber, E.: Key Lessons from Standish's 2015 Chaos Report (2015). http://www.erikweber-consulting.com/blog/chaos2015. Accessed: 23 Aug 2022
27. Yvonne Schoper und Anja Viehbacher (leads): Individual Competence Baseline für Projektmanagement Version 4.0 Deutsche Fassung. GPM Deutsche Gesellschaft für Projektmanagement e.V. (2017). URL https://www.gpm-ipma.de/know_how/pm_normen_und_standards/standard_icb_4.html. Accessed: 23 Aug 2022

Cross-Sectional Themes

2

The goal of this chapter is to give you an overview of the topics that are important throughout the entire duration of a project. The following sections deal with requirements, change management, project culture, communication, documentation, quality, risk management, and methods.

At the end of this chapter, you will have learned and understood all project-spanning topics.

2.1 Requirements

"If you want a wise answer, you must ask a reasonable question."

Johann Wolfgang von Goethe (1749–1832) This section provides an overview of the relationship between requirements and projects in general. Requirements in the context of agile software development are considered in Sect. 4.2.2. According to Pohl and Rupp [17], requirements engineering includes the identification, documentation, coordination, and management of requirements. Experts have come together in this field to train and certify [11]. At the end of this section, you will know how to identify and manage requirements.

2.1.1 The Goal of Requirements Engineering

The goal of requirements engineering is to achieve a shared understanding of a product or system to be developed with complete and clear requirements [10]. Good requirements engineering helps to avoid errors or detect and fix them early. This can save the cost of late error correction. Requirements engineering takes into account the different experience and knowledge levels of the project participants. For this purpose, the requirements of the relevant stakeholders are recorded, analyzed, documented and

© Springer-Verlag GmbH Germany, part of Springer Nature 2022
D. Alam and U. Gühl, *Project Management for Practice*,
https://doi.org/10.1007/978-3-662-65159-9_2

validated in high quality. Stakeholders in this context are all those who can influence the project, are interested in the project or are affected by the project.

2.1.2   Projects and Requirements

The expected project results are based on requirements. As listed in Sect. 1.2, the importance of requirements arises from the fact that the main reasons for failed software projects are changing or poorly documented requirements. In general, at the beginning of any project it is crucial to determine the requirements for the product or system and to coordinate and agree on these with the client as well as the project environment. This often avoids confusion and discrepancies in the interpretation of general requirements. The goal is also to detect conflicts or contradictions between individual requirements, clarify the wishes of the stakeholders and obtain clear, solution-neutral requirements.

The requirements recorded initially can change during the course of the project: some may be dropped, others may be added. This results in the need to constantly revise the requirements, to reduce or expand them as needed and to keep them as conflict-free as possible.

Requirements Engineering
Requirements Engineering includes the following topics [17]:

- *Requirements definition*
  The requirements of the stakeholders are to be identified, documented and coordinated.
- *Requirements management*
  The captured requirements are to be managed and, if necessary, changed consistently.

Requirements can change. Possible causes are described in Sect. 2.2.2. Requirements Engineering helps to deal with requirements and their changes professionally.

2.1.3   Capturing Requirements

To capture the requirements, it is most useful to first consult the client. A project order with target definition should be available. The wishes and ideas of the client should be known.

In addition to the requirements specified by the client, consider possible additional sources for project requirements (see Fig. 2.1). If a product or service is being developed as part of the project, the Kano model shown in Fig. 2.2 can also help with the capture of requirements [14].

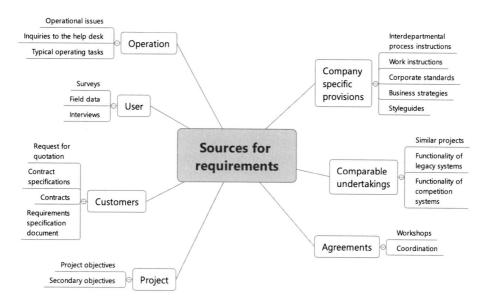

Fig. 2.1   Sources of requirements

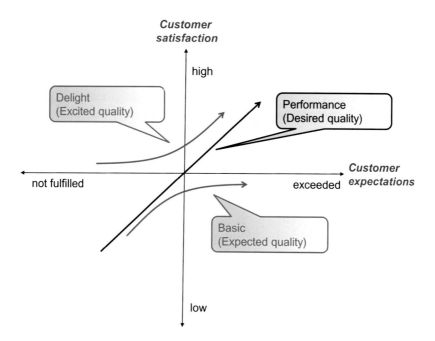

Fig. 2.2   Kano model

The Kano model measures customer satisfaction with the classification of product features into:

- Basic features
  Implicit customer expectations are often not mentioned, but assumed as a matter of course (example: existing air conditioning in new vehicles).
- Performance features
  These can be specified and often serve as distinguishing criteria for comparable products (example: screen size, resolution and energy consumption for TVs).
- Delight features
  A "wow effect" is something that a customer does not expect and can contribute to high customer satisfaction (example: gesture control when smartphones are introduced).

Delight features change over time to become basic features. For example, the highly innovative anti-lock braking system ABS, which was available for the Mercedes-Benz S-Class W116 in 1978, is now a basic feature of passenger cars. The Kano model teaches that basic features must not be ignored. In addition, specific delight features can be achieved if the respective customer requirements are known.

When developing products or services, users or potential customers should be involved in defining project requirements, for example in the form of surveys, workshops, provision of prototypes or participation in a test phase. The aim should be to turn those affected into participants. Furthermore, there are data collection techniques such as field observation or research into documents in the project context, for example descriptions of old systems, competitor systems or similar applications. Identified requirements for a project are to be documented in the next step. This can be done in natural language, but also model-based. In this case, reality is modelled by a set of graphical elements. The INVEST model helps to check whether requirements are well formulated [24].

INVEST stands for following terms with the meaning:

- **I**ndependent—no dependencies on other requirements
- **N**egotiable—contains the essentials, not too detailed
- **V**aluable—has value for a user
- **E**stimable—helps with planning and prioritization
- **S**mall—manageable scope, which can be implemented within a foreseeable time frame
- **T**estable—to test the implementation of a requirement

Finally, the requirements are checked and agreed to by the stakeholders. A template for capturing requirements in the form of a requirements list can be found in Sect. 6.3 on page 160. Also helpful is a project glossary to avoid misunderstandings in the requirements. It should contain abbreviations and technical terms with their meaning (see also page 30).

2.1.4   Managing Requirements

Requirements management[1] is a continuous process throughout the entire project duration. Managing requirements includes the following activities:

- Documentation
  Requirements are provided with attributes such as name, description, author, criticality or priority.
- Prioritization
  The prioritization determines the weighting and sequence of requirements. It is carried out depending on the distribution of roles in the project by the client, by the department or by the project manager.
- Change tracking
  During the project, new requirements may arise, existing ones may change or be dropped. The respective changes are to be recorded. It must be ensured that requirements and requirement changes can be traced throughout the project. This way it is known from which source a requirement originates, which stakeholder has made a requirement and which events or reasons led to changes.
- Transparency
  The status of the requirements must be transparent to the stakeholders in the project. The stakeholders should have easy access to the requirements.
- Dealing with requirements changes
  - Suggestions
    Requirements change requests can come from all stakeholders and are to be documented accordingly.
  - Analysis
    In order to assess the effort and impact of a requirements change request, an analysis is necessary. For this purpose, cost estimates and expert recommendations are recommended.
  - Coordination and approval
    For accepted requirements change request, the priority of implementation is set.

Further information on dealing with changes to requirements can be found in Sect. 2.2.3.

2.2   Change Management

"If you want to be always happy, you often have to change."
  Confucius (probably 551–479 BC) A project does not stand alone, but has interactions with the environment. The larger a project is and the longer it takes, the more intense the interactions. If key parameters in the environment change, a project must be able to react

---

[1] In the literature, requirements management is sometimes equated with requirements engineering.

flexible. Changes occur. These are legitimate and can also be seen as an opportunity. So it's not about avoiding changes in a project, but about dealing with them professionally. Possible reasons for changes can be found in Fig. 2.3.

Above all, the client needs transparency about the consequences. That is, will change requests result in additional costs, delays or additional complexity?

Change
In the context of project management, DIN 69901-5 specifies a "change justified by a change request, implemented by a change decision and confirmed as implemented by a change notification of previously valid documents (plans, contracts, etc.)" [6].

Change Management
Change management is, according to DIN 69901-5, the "recording, evaluation, decision-making, documentation and control of the implementation of changes in the project in relation to the previously valid planning" [6]. The aim is the timely planning and implementation of changes on schedule.

2.2.1 Goals of Change Management

Changes should essentially lead to a better project result, based on new or changed requirements, discovered errors or new findings. Changes can also reduce costs and effort. Plans that have been created once need to be adapted. With the help of a common understanding and a uniform change management process between the project participants, changes should be coordinated and implemented in a targeted manner. A targeted change management should prevent "worsening improvements". These are changes that do not lead to improvements, but to deterioration due to effects that were not considered.

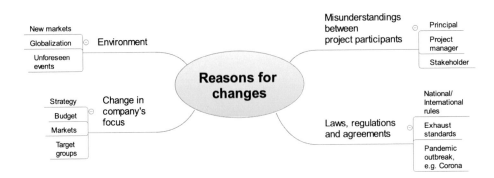

Fig. 2.3 Possible reasons for changes

The "cobra effect" is an example [23]: In India, a snake plague was to be combatted by offering a reward for each specimen killed. This worked at first with the delivery of ever more dead snakes. However, the total number of snakes did not decrease, as eventually cobras were bred and killed for the reward.

2.2.2   Causes of Change

In small projects, up to 25% of requirements change, in large projects this can be up to 50% [22]. The average change rate of requirements for software projects is about 2% per month, though depending on the product context there is a variance of about 1 to 4% [15, p. 372]. Various reasons for changes in industry and commerce also affect specific projects. For example [21]: during the development of a vehicle, a supplier presents an innovative lighting concept. This is closer to the color spectrum of daylight than previous solutions, which strains the driver's eyes less. In addition, the developed solution has a very low energy consumption, which saves up to 0.05 l of fuel per 100 km. The car manufacturer decides to implement the developed lighting concept as part of a change.

2.2.3   Scope of Change Management

Change management is an important cross-functional activity of project management. It affects the entire project cycle, including:

- Requirements
  Changed requirements, e.g. regarding missing functionality, are the most important source of changes in the project. Therefore, they must be handled professionally.
- Quality
  Required certifications, increased quality requirements or identified quality problems, such as technological problems or system malfunctions, lead to changes in projects.
- Risk management
  What may happen during a project is not always foreseeable. With the help of a risk analysis (see Sect. 2.7), it is possible to identify preventive measures. Their implementation can lead to changes in the project.
- Project planning
  Even if changes are not foreseeable from the outset, activities such as the estimation of the cost of changes, the establishment of a change process or the installation of a change committee can be planned.
- Project control
  The professional handling of changes is a key activity in project implementation.

Depending on the size and structure of the project, change management is carried out by individual roles or committees. In principle, the project manager is responsible for change management. He can carry out change management alone or with defined stakeholders. Another possibility is the establishment of a change manager with a change committee. A change committee like a Change Control Board (CCB) is responsible as a change committee for whether changes are accepted and in which priority they are processed. Typical members of the CCB are the client, the project manager, customer or user representatives, the change managerand key stakeholders. A change management process ensures that changes are coordinated.

Figure 2.4 shows a simple change management process with the following steps:

- Capture
  Change requests can be made by all stakeholders in principle. Depending on the organization, change requests are created with a document or in a system. The following should be included:
  – Heading with unique change number
  – Change description, possibly with visualization or explanatory attachments
  – Initiator
  – Reasons for the change
  – Effort estimation
  – Dependencies
  – Status
  – Priority
  – Responsible for implementation
  – Implementation date, by when the implementation should be completed
- Detail
  The proposed changes are formulated and should cover all aspects as much as possible. For this purpose, the project members concerned are usually involved.
- Evaluate
  Advantages and disadvantages are weighed up and substantiated with arguments. Cost and time aspects are shown. The result is a decision template for management.
- Reconcile and approve
  How changes are approved depends on the organization of change management as described above. It is important to document the respective decisions on a change request, preferably with the decision-makers and a justification.

Fig. 2.4 Example of a change management process

- Implement

    After approval, the change is implemented. Configuration management ensures that all changes made to the resulting project result are traceable.

The scope and effort for change management depends on the complexity and size of the project. The biggest challenge is financing approved changes, as they are often not included in the project budget. In smaller projects, it is possible to take into account certain change volumes already during planning in the form of a buffer.

2.2.4 Change Management and Agility

In agile methodology, change management is automatically integrated. One of the basic principles of agility is: Expect changes. This makes dealing with changes much easier than with traditional projects. By involving the customers, they have the opportunity to prioritize at regular intervals whether the focus should be on new functionality or necessary changes. This can avoid a costly change management. In case of volatile requirements or projects where the exact requirements are not clear at the beginning, an agile approach is recommended, see Chap. 4.

2.3 Project Culture

"If you want to build a ship, don't drum up people to gather wood, divide the work and give orders. Instead, teach them to yearn for the vast and endless sea."

Antoine de Saint-Exupery (1900–1944) This section shows the connection between successful projects and a good project culture. In addition, there is information on how to create a good working atmosphere. There is a close connection to the areas of communication (see Sect. 2.4) and social competence. Every project develops its own project culture. This is expressed in how cooperation is organized in the project, whether there is a common understanding of roles, how errors are dealt with in the project, which methodology is used and which rules apply in the project. Due to globalization, there are more and more international projects. Here, special attention should be paid to dealing with cultural differences, different values and a common language in the project.

2.3.1 Goals of the Project Culture

A good project culture ensures that all team members can work together on the common goal as best as possible. The most important part of the project culture includes the respectful, appreciative and trusting treatment of the people involved in the project.

Project Culture
The project culture can be defined as the "totality of the behavior of the project participants influenced by knowledge, experience and tradition and the general assessment of this behavior by the project environment" [1]. The project culture includes the soft skills in the project, for example:

- Identification with the project
- Willingness to cooperate internally and externally
- Fairness and respect
- Communication skills
- Conflict management
- Activity level for the project
- Openness

2.3.2 Outward Effect of a Project

"Nothing good happens unless you do it."
  Erich Kästner (1899–1974) A project is not in a vacuum. For example, there is an affected public in infrastructure projects. In corporate projects, there are affected areas in the company that are not involved. Often this environment has a certain influence on a project (see Sect. 3.1.3), so the best possible representation of the project to the outside world is required:

- Look for allies, for instance within the organization, who support the project—for example as a sponsor.
- In addition, your goal must be: make people concerned become people involved. People have to work on the upcoming tasks together.
  - For example, if an end user is involved in the design, she will find it easier to cope with future changes in the workflow.
  - If the operation is involved in the development of software, it will operate the finished IT product with higher motivation.
  This can result in cooperation in specific cases.
- Identify possible sources of conflict or the need for action and take appropriate measures. These can be different religions of project members, differences in the way women and men are treated, in work and eating culture, etc.
- Involve stakeholders in your project, at least through regular information.
- Always present the results of the project in time and show the highlights to interested circles and personalities who can support your project, for example in bilateral talks.
- Hold regular events, such as a forum, where you actively inform about the project. Take in the feedback, criticism or questions that arise.

- Advertise your project.

The following points not only help to present a project to outsiders, but also make it easier for project members to identify with the project:

- Project vision
  This allows the project employees to have a shared understanding and provides motivation to work together towards a common project goal.
- Descriptive project name
- Good interpersonal climate
- Project glossary
- Project logo
- Tandem principle
  Someone in the project forms a tandem with someone outside the project, e.g. with an end user, in order to capture requirements and receive expert advice (schematic representation in Fig. 2.7 on page 31).

2.3.3 Inwards Effect of a Project

"It is better to have the respect of mankind at all times than their admiration occasionally."
   Jean-Jacques Rousseau (1712–1778) One of the most important things in the project is the way we treat each other: We appreciate and respect each other. We work with people in the project. The cooperation in the team is the basis for the success of the project. All project employees should stand behind the project and be convinced of the sense of the project. It is the enduring task of the project manager to motivate and convince. A good first step to involve all project members is the project kickoff (see Sect. 3.2.9). A successful project culture includes the self-responsibility of the project employees. If the project members identify with their tasks, which they design independently, they identify more easily with the overall project. Therefore, project employees should be given clear tasks with measurable goals that can be solved independently. In a review, the work results can be evaluated and suggestions for improvement can be worked out for the future. How can you motivate your project employees to do a good job in the project?

- Give clear tasks with clear responsibilities.
- Define with measurable goals when a task is complete.
- Prioritize the tasks.
- Consider the interests of the project members when distributing tasks. Remember, what someone likes to do, is what he will do well.
- Support self-dependent work.
  Let the responsible person specify or change the task. They are often closer to the topic and can correctly classify it.
  Don't ask when the task will be done?
  Ask what will be done by a certain date?
- Feedback culture

Regular feedback can help the project member for personal development. Opportunities could be the completion of work packages or project milestones.
- Conflict management
  As a project manager, make sure you have good conflict management. Avoid unnecessary conflicts.
  For example, if a project member does not want to take on a certain task, it is better to ask if someone else will take on the task than to force the project member to do the work.
- Keep your project employees productive.
  Free your project employees of any obstacles that hinder them—such as avoidable bureaucratic or administrative activities.
- Efficient project meetings
  Ensure an adequate but not too large number of project meetings. Each project meeting should have a clear goal that is clearly formulated at the beginning. Only those who can actively contribute should participate.
- Make sure that the tasks assigned are challenging.
- Show your project employees professional perspectives.
- Regularly inform about the status of the project.
- "Eating your own dog food"
  Use programs or tools that you create for customers in your own project or in your own company.

Prominently display information about the project and the status of the project, for example as a poster with the project goals or project results. Visualize the project rules in meeting rooms on a flipchart. Make sure you have good working conditions so that your project employees can work optimally and for a pleasant atmosphere in the project. Examples:

- Define common rules
- Small delicacies, snacks, pretzels and drinks for meetings
- Setting up a fruit bowl
  Here project members can eat healthily and exchange information.
- Project events such as the visit of cultural events or common sport activities
- Common project breakfast

2.3.4   Decision Culture

"At some point you have to take the leap into the unknown. First, because even the right decision is wrong if it is made too late. Second, because in most cases there is no such thing as certainty."
    Lee Iacocca (1924–2019) A project manager regularly has to make decisions. Project managers who are decision-makers are usually also successful. However, a project manager does not always decide alone. There are dependencies, in particular to the client and to the

steering group, but also some stakeholders can have a very large influence on a project. Furthermore, the organizational form (see Sect. 3.2.6) plays a major role in the decision-making powers of a project manager. Decisions that need to be made because of dependencies, but are not made can be problematic. These can paralyze a project or bring it to a standstill in the worst case.

Example: In an IT project, the budget for a desired source code change has not yet been released. The tests should only start when the software is finished—with or without the source code change being carried out. Since the project manager does not want to take the risk of commissioning the changes without financial security on the one hand, but on the other hand does not want to do without the changes, she waits. This blocks the tests.

The following thought on project philosophy: Do not be afraid of wrong decisions. It is easier to ask for forgiveness than for permission. Establish a decision-making culture in your project. You can achieve this with the following measures:

- Transfer of responsibility
  The decision-making powers in the project are transferred to the sub-projects and people responsible for work packages with regard to their areas of work. They are to act independently and decide within their area of responsibility. These design options promote self-responsibility, strengthen the self-confidence of the project members and thus enable efficient work in the project.
- What has been decided should not be discussed again.
  Exception: Awareness of new, previously not considered facts.
- Automatic approval
  Often, urgent decisions are needed, but the corresponding decision-making bodies do not meet in time. Here, it can be agreed after prior consultation that objections to a pre-formulated decision are possible until a deadline has expired. If no objections are received by then, the decision shall be deemed to have been taken without further resolution. This procedure ensures that a project is not blocked for days or even weeks due to a missing decision. Example: After the completion of a preliminary project, a special software tool is to be introduced.
- Decisions and resolutions made are documented and made transparent for all project participants. This can be done, for example, in a digital project handbook. Figure 2.5 shows another example. Decisions can be listed in a list. The corresponding file can be stored in a project drive that is accessible to all project members.

2.3.5   Learning in the Project

"Two things are needed for our work: tireless endurance and the willingness to throw away something that one has put a lot of time and work into."
   Albert Einstein (1879–1955) Use the capacities in the team to become better in the project, learn constantly in the project. Make sure that knowledge is exchanged in your project and that project members can replace each other. Avoid too much dependence on individual

No.	Decision	Responsible	Date	Remarks
1	The book will be written using LaTeX	Gühl	16-06-2021	
2	For the book cover SVI_FA_MAS_T05 is used	Alam	12-07-2022	Mail exchange with Springer
3				

Fig. 2.5 Example of a list of decisions

project members. There should not be a bottleneck focused on one person, so that the project fails if this specific person is missing. Support an open atmosphere in which mistakes can be made. Handle errors positively:

- Errors are legitimate: Whoever works makes mistakes.
- Known errors are good—unknown errors are not good
  Known errors can be corrected and learned from. And you can take precautions so that they don't happen again in the future.
- Every error we fix now saves future costs and secures project success.
- No finger-pointing. Instead work in a solution-oriented way: how can we correct errors together?

Establish regular dates in the project to stop and reflect with your project team: Where are we? What went well? What should have gone better? What can we do? This corresponds to the PDCA cycle according to Deming [5] with the steps Plan, Do, Check, Act (see Sect. 2.6).

The Scrum software development method provides regular retrospectives in which good and improvement-worthy points are addressed and discussed (see Sect. 4.2.6). The goal is to establish a culture of change and to work better with the implementation of proposals for improvements in the project.

If your project is growing dynamically, introduce a "mentor principle" in which experienced project members take care of new project members and accompany their first time in the project. Furthermore, exchanging with other projects can be helpful, as well as accessing a company knowledge base with information about projects (see Sect. 3.4.3).

2.3.6 International Projects

The more global the networking in the world becomes, the more important the cultural aspect becomes in international projects. If people from different cultural circles come together in a project, the corresponding differences, for example, concerning values, have to be considered. Also language differences are not to be neglected. The predominant language in international projects is English, but not all project members have the same level of experience in English. Therefore the risk of misunderstandings increases. It is recommended to carry out an intercultural training in order to better understand aspects of foreign cultures in an international project and to avoid misunderstandings. Language courses can help improve communication. Regardless of this: respectful treatment is always right. The internationalization of a project naturally results in an additional complexity level due to different languages, cultures, project locations and possibly time differences.

2.3.7 Projects During the COVID-19 Pandemic

The worldwide Corona pandemic, which has been developing since January 2020, has had a massive impact on society as a whole, on working life and thus also on projects. The projects of the authors have also been and are very much influenced by the Corona crisis. The restrictions imposed as part of the measures to combat the pandemic with contact and exit restrictions, closures of universities, schools, nurseries and certain businesses, quarantine regulations, social distancing rules, mask wearing, etc. have resulted in enormous burdens for many people. In particular, the domestic care of children and young people parallel to work in the home office often proved to be very difficult.

However, there were also positive aspects to these measures—at least for some groups of people. Working from home saves time because there are no commuting costs. A home office can enable relaxed and concentrated work and make it easier to combine family and work. Job satisfaction is also higher because self-determined and flexible work is possible. It is striking that in video and audio conferences project members tend to deal with each other more attentively. The following measures and rules have proven to be effective:

1. Health and safety come first
   In the company, social distancing and hygiene rules should be planned and implemented, for example with easy access to disinfectants. Project members should stay at home if they have any symptoms of illness.
2. Ensure communication
   The principles discussed in Sect. 2.4 apply even more in virtual projects. It is not possible to talk to each other directly on site or to go to the desk of a project employee. Therefore, the project manager is even more responsible for ensuring communication in the project. The following tips and hints:
   - Arrange regular, preferably daily, short appointments so that project information can be distributed and difficulties can be identified in good time (compare with Daily Scrum on page 142).

- If several people are working intensively on a topic, a coordination meeting should take place in the morning. The progress can then be discussed at noon and the results summarized and consolidated in the afternoon.
- Promote collaboration in small teams or in pairs (compare explanations of the tandem principle on page 31).
- Ensure transparency with easy access to project-relevant information and tools.

3. Keep project members productive
   The home office must be sufficiently technically equipped. In case of problems with the infrastructure, support must be guaranteed.

4. Knowledge transfer
   In projects, it is often also about transferring and sharing knowledge, for example in the form of work results. This is challenging if you cannot simply go to a meeting room with several people and start spontaneously. If the project members are internationally distributed and only virtual meetings are possible, for example in the form of a video conference, the following procedure is recommended:
   - Distribute materials in advance and ask participants for questions in advance. Then answer these during the appointment.
   - Convey the knowledge in the video conference using documents and presentations.
   - Address listeners directly during the conference.
   - Assign (smaller) tasks and have a participant present a solution proposal.
   - Ask (simple) comprehension questions to ensure that participants can still follow.
   - Give room for feedback again and again.
   - Clear break rules for appointments that last longer than one hour.
   - At the end of the appointment, ask for feedback from the participants.

5. Focus on planning and control
   When working remotely, project management is challenging. Thus, good planning with task structuring and prioritization, and clear responsibilities, is even more important in virtual projects.
   Likewise, project control with monitoring of project progress is more demanding. The project manager should consciously focus on these points and delegate other tasks as far as possible. The project manager must trust the project team here and let the project team know.

2.3.8   Failure

"Always tried. Always failed. No matter. Try again. Fail again. Fail better."
   Samuel Beckett (1906–1989) A difficult question is how to deal with bad news when the project is in danger of failing or has failed. There is no simple clear answer that fits every situation.

When in doubt, the following rule should apply: Be authentic and honest, and stand by (your own) weaknesses. One's own project should **never** be whitewashed. A failure should also be admitted in good time. The responsible persons must be able to understand the project situation and make corresponding decisions. Therefore, in this case, you should talk to the client or decision-makers in good time. Reasons for the project's poor performance should also be identified here, as these offer approaches for changes or possibilities for improvement. Instead of criticism, one often receives surprisingly helpful and supportive assistance.

In general, a failure at an early stage is cheaper than a failure at a later stage. Regular project reviews—see Sect. 2.6.2—can counter a failure at a later stage. The corporate culture plays a very important role in this context. The more critical a failure is seen in the project environment, for example, when team members lose prestige, the more self-confident a project manager must be to admit a failure. In the worst case, it leads to very high costs if a project is not stopped in time.

2.3.9   Checklist

Figure 2.6 shows a checklist for the project culture.

Checklist project culture

Project name		Project no.	
Responsible			
Version / Date		Status	

Question	Result
1. Is it assured that the project culture will continuously be adapted and improved as and when required?	
2. Is it clear which decisions are taken by the project manager and which by the project members?	
3. Is it assured that the project members could work on their own responsibility?	
4. Do the project members jointly accept decisions, even if there are single opinions?	
5. Are issues raised and promptly discussed and solved?	
6. Are rules of the game defined, and do all project members follow them?	
7. Is positive or negative criticism jointly accepted to improve?	
8. Is clear who is supporting whom and who should be asked in case of issues?	

Fig. 2.6   Checklist project culture

2.4   Communication

"You cannot not communicate."
  Paul Watzlawick (1921–2007) Communication means exchange or transfer of information and is essential for projects. Only in this way is a goal-oriented cooperation possible. It is vital that information arrives with the participants. The importance of communication therefore lies in its effect, not in its intention.

2.4.1   Goals of Communication

The goals of communication are:

- Clear transfer of content and ideas, in order to be able to understand even complex matters.
- Exchange of different viewpoints.
- Clarification of interpersonal and factual differences.
- Reporting, adapted to the respective requirements of the recipients.

Good communication supports and influences a project decisively. It can have an impact on the following areas (see also Sect. 2.3):

- Mutual respect. Project members listen to each other and let each other finish.
- Common understanding that leads to common action.
- Transparency, which, for example, leads to better understanding of decisions and can build trust.
- Identifying and resolving conflicts.

Communication in the Project
Communication in the project represents the exchange of information between the project participants, especially within the project team, and is a key success factor. The communication plan specifies who communicates with whom and how often in the project. Distinguish between verbal and nonverbal communication. Communication difficulties due to cultural differences are particularly possible in international projects.

2.4.2   Aspects of Communication

From the very beginning, people communicate with each other, they want to be understood. Communication consists of:

- Verbal elements
  These are the linguistic content.
- Nonverbal elements
  These include gestures, facial expressions, body language and voice.

With the nonverbal part of communication, in addition to the linguistic content, additional information is exchanged such as emotional states, wishes or expectations of the conversation partner. Especially body language and facial expressions stand for the credibility of a statement. According to a study by Mehrabian and Ferris [16], the following applies to presentations to groups:

- 55% of the effect is achieved through body language, i.e. posture, gestures, and eye contact.
- 38% of the effect is achieved through acoustic impressions such as voice and tone.
- 7% of the effect is achieved through the content of the presentation.

In communication, the following must also be distinguished:

- Congruent behavior
  Verbal and nonverbal content match.
- Incongruent behavior
  Verbal and nonverbal content do not match.
  Example: A project employee assures that she "likes to write the protocol very much". But her face and gestures show rejection and reluctance: statement and external behavior do not match.

The nonverbal part is by far the larger part of the information. A possible conclusion: If the nonverbal part is perceived as true, the entire information is interpreted as true.

It should be noted that communication is generally prone to error. Information can be simplified or even incorrect, which can lead to misunderstandings or rumors. This must be taken into account in planning. The challenge, especially in international projects, is often the difficulty of exchanging information in a common language.

2.4.3 Good Communication

Good communication is characterized by:

- Appreciation and recognition
  Respect your conversation partner and let him know.
- Active listening
  Repeat what you have heard in your own words. Ask if you do not understand. Ask your conversation partner to repeat what he understood.
- Open questions

Open questions cannot be answered with "yes" or "no". They therefore serve as an incentive for an exchange. Open questions show your conversation partner that you are interested and make it easier for him to engage in a particular topic. Example: How can we optimize the print?

- Praise
  Praise is a special form of appreciation: praise what is concrete and well-founded, for example, if an employee is very committed and has achieved a very good result.
- I-messages
  Give your own thoughts and opinions, for example: "I did not like how you dealt with the customer", instead of "You can not deal with the customer like that."
- Addressing specific situations or specific behavior
  Refer to specific facts such as "You sent me the wrong document". Avoid general statements like "You're doing everything wrong". Address problems directly and as soon as possible.
- Focus
  Stay on topic, don't wander off. Try to finalize a discussion on a subject.

2.4.4 Communication as a Task for the Project Manager

"Nature has given us only one mouth, but two ears, which suggests that we should speak less and listen more."

   Zenon, Greek philosopher (c. 490–430 BC) The above comments imply the importance of communication. The efficient internal exchange of information between all project stakeholders is one of the key success factors for a project. Approximately 90% of good project management work involves communication [19]. Communication is a (if not the) key to project success. Tom DeMarco, established project management author and inventor of "structured analysis", writes: "Projects do not fail because of the technology, but because of the people" (according to [4]). Michael Campbell surveyed over 500 project managers. The most important success factor mentioned was communication. In projects that failed, communication was always identified as a critical factor [3]. A project manager always has to stay on the ball. She must have an overview of her project; she always needs to know what is happening. In order for this to be ensured, a good project culture and good communication are necessary. Specifically:

- Communicate actively
  Keep an ear out for your project employees. Have personal conversations. Actively ask about progress and problems in the project, but also about the personal situation: How are you?
- Always be approachable
  Make sure that people can easily get in touch with you. Set up appointments that you are definitely available for. If the premises allow it, choose your workplace directly in the project team; in the middle instead of on the outside.
- Lead by example

As a project manager, understand that your own behavior is an example for the project employees and has a significant impact on the external image of the project.

- Promote team building in the project through the tandem principle.
  Form pairs in your teams, e.g. one person works, the other checks. Mentors take care of new project members. Developers and testers work as a tandem. This is also useful in communication with the outside world, for example a pair formation with experts from departments or end users. Mix the pairs regularly. Figure 2.7 schematically shows the tandem principle.
- Create a calm atmosphere as well
  Too much or constant communication is not always good. For example, it takes about 15 minutes to get involved in a complex topic. Disturbances every fifteen minutes ensure that there is no productivity. Separate offices and measures such as meeting-free days are suitable here.
- Work actively to improve communication
  Communication can be improved, with a positive attitude towards the project, and empathy and appreciation for all project participants. Increasing the quality of communication means increasing the quality of cooperation in the project. Set rules if necessary.
- Shape the atmosphere in the project
  Good manners, consistent attitudes and open, transparent communication enable a pleasant, work-promoting atmosphere.
- Talk to people directly
  Look for a personal conversation instead of checking the status by email or anonymous status reports. Use tools like email consciously. Prevent "mail ping pong". In general, such emails take up a lot of time and do not really contribute to finding a solution. Rather, use the phone or go to the person's workplace. If you discuss something, it is recommended to summarize it in an email that reflects the most important agreements of the conversation.

Fig. 2.7 Schematic representation of the tandem principle

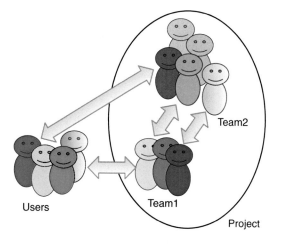

- Carry out regular meetings
  Use these meetings so that project members can express themselves about the project. Important topics are the current status and risks in the project. Involve the team members in providing contributions. Clarify the contributions in advance. Send an agenda with time limits in advance, which you adhere to during the meeting. Only at the end of the term do you have the opportunity to raise further points.
- Clear communication
  When tasks arise, they should be distributed directly. Who does what by when? Choose a project member who appears to be suitable for a specific task and address them directly. "Somebody should …" leaves tasks open, shows decision-making problems, delays problem solving and thus appears demotivating.
- Use of a glossary
  Different understandings of terms can lead to conflicts in projects. For organizations and domains there are always specific glossaries that are intended to facilitate communication and collaboration, such as in software development [8] or software testing [13]. The introduction of a glossary that defines all project-relevant terms is also recommended for projects. It should be ensured that only one glossary is valid in the project, that it is regularly maintained and that it is accessible to all project members [17]. A glossary also helps in dealing with requirements (Sect. 2.1).

Successful projects are characterized by many opportunities for information and communication among project participants. Sometimes it makes sense not to always use the hierarchy, but also to establish direct contacts through cross-connections. Bring people together, pass on targeted information. Get the project members talking to each other. Create opportunities for communication such as a fruit bowl or a coffee machine. Knowledge increases when it is shared. On the one hand, it should be ensured that the project manager informs specifically (see Sect. 2.4.5), on the other hand, it should also be ensured that diverse communication within the project team is possible. From the above explanations, it also makes sense that a project team works together at one location. So there should be no spatial separation of the team. If project members are located at different sites, a temporary solution with regular meetings may help. Example: The project team meets every two weeks for one week at one location.

2.4.5 Communication Plan

Synonyms for the communication plan are *communication model* or *information management*. The communication of the project inward (internal communication) and outward (external communication) should be planned and regulated. For this purpose a communication plan is required. In this, it is recorded who receives which information at what time and how the project participants get the information they need for their work.

In addition, the communication plan shows the escalation process that is triggered in case of conflicts in the project. Example: communication of decisions of the steering committee[2] with publication of the protocol in a special place, preferably with the possibility to search there. The communication plan should be created early in the project and include communication with all stakeholders. It is usually based on the project organization (see Sect. 3.2.6). Transparency in the project is a success factor when all relevant information is available to every project participant, so that everyone can access it quickly and easily. Ideally, these access records are stored in the project manual.

Figure 2.8 shows a communication plan. The corresponding template can be found in Sect. 6.6 on page 170. The following explanations apply:

- Project client meetings
  Schedule regular meetings with the client.
- Steering committee meetings
  Schedule regular meetings and reviews with the steering committee.
- Project meetings
  Include a regular communication with your project team in your communication plan. For larger projects, this may be the project core team. Note: Regular communication is a planned, recurring meeting, for example, every Friday at 2:00 p.m. These dates are then referred to as, for example, a regular communication or Jour fixe (regular meeting).
- Bilateral communication
  Try to have a personal conversation with each project member at regular intervals.
- Additional meetings
  Depending on the type of project, there may be topic-specific professional meetings.
- External Communication
  Depending on the project, "external" may mean different things. In a large company, this may be the organization, in a public project the population. Possible options for a communication strategy include:
  - Regular communication with sponsors.
  - Project forum: The topics of the project are presented to interested colleagues in the company once a month.

In addition, informal communication should not be underestimated. Project-decisive communication does not necessarily take place in the meetings provided for this purpose.

---

[2] Steering committee is explained on page 96.

Communication plan

Project name	*<Name of project>*	Project No.	*<Number of project>*
Project manager	*<Name of project manager>*		
Version / Date	*<0.1 / Day.Month.Year>*	Status	*<initiated, in progress, done, cancelled>*
Author	*<Name of author>*		

Kind of communication	Who/ With whom	Purpose	Frequency	Comments
<Principal meetings>	*<Principal>*	*<Update, critical issues, approval requests>*	*<Biweekly, on request>*	*<Comments>*
<Project board meetings>	*<Project board>*	*<Status, approval requests>*	*<Every two months>*	*<Comments>*
<Project meetings>	*<Project members>*	*<Status, critical issues, risks>*	*<Weekly>*	*<Comments>*
<Core project meetings>	*<Core project members>*	*<Status, next steps, issues>*	*<Daily>*	*<Comments>*
<Status report>	*<Principal, project board, project members>*	*<General information>*	*<Monthly>*	*<Comments>*

Fig. 2.8 Template communication plan with hints

2.4.6 Project Meetings

Project meetings offer opportunities, but also risks. They provide opportunities to inform participants, collect good ideas and work productively to advance the project. Risks due to inefficient meetings include valuable time lost with no clear results. Make sure you moderate meetings with a large number of people. The more complex the topic and the more different the interests of the participants are, the more important moderation becomes. The following rules for project meetings are recommended:

- Determine the right group of people
- Set up an agenda with agenda items and predetermined times.
  Distinguish each:
  - Information
  - Discussion
  - Decisions requests/decisions
Agree on the agenda items with the affected persons in advance. Consider time differences in international meetings.
- Sending the invitation with the agenda in a timely manner
  Depending on the topic and the target group, "in good time" can mean several weeks or just a few days. The more important the topic and the more extensive the participants' preliminary work, the earlier the invitation should be sent. It is also possible to send a placeholder invitation first and then to provide details later ("Save the date").
- Define roles
  It is recommended to appoint a moderator and a scribe, especially for larger meetings.
- Observe times
  The specified times must be adhered to during the meeting. The moderator is responsible for this. In exceptional cases, items can be postponed or extended at the expense of other items. However, this should be decided consciously and not happen at random.
- Document decisions and tasks
  Please note: Without minutes, a meeting has not taken place! If possible, take minutes or have a scribe take minutes during the meeting and use the time at the end of the meeting to go through the minutes together. This saves or at least reduces subsequent effort for corrections, for example due to misunderstandings or forgotten points.

The task list has proven itself effective for the logging of project meetings. In addition to information, such as results presented and resolutions made, different tasks are usually assigned as results of project meetings. Keep track of these in a task list, each with a responsible person and target date by which the task should be completed. This then results in an overview of the tasks to be completed in the project. If there is a regular update, the task list always contains the open points in the project at the current time. An example of a task list is shown in Fig. 2.9. A template is available in Sect. 6.2 on page 159.

No.	Task	Category	Priority	Responsible	Start date	Target date	Status	Result	Remarks
1	Check links in the bibliography and update them	Book 3rd edition	high	Gühl	03-05-2023	19-07-2023	done	In version 0.9 links are updated	
2	Select cover and inform Springer	Book 3rd edition	medium	Alam	05-07-2023	31-07-2023	in progress		First phone call conducted
3	Thank you message to reviewer	Book 3rd edition	low	Gühl	10-06-2024	30-09-2024	planned		
4									

Fig. 2.9   Example of a task list

Figure 2.10 shows a minutes template with hints. The corresponding minutes template can be found in Sect. 6.7 on page 172. Note: If complex topics, alternative solutions, etc. are discussed in a session, it is recommended to attach the corresponding documents as separate documents in the appendix.

2.4.7   Communication Tools

In addition to natural communication with language and technical communication with documents and electronic media, use novel communication tools to make your project known. Use marketing measures to promote your project—there can never be enough supporters. Your imagination is the only limit here. Examples:

- Conferences,[3] professional meetings, support of working groups
- Flyers, brochures
- Posters
- Advertising materials such as cups, pens, bottle openers, blocks, T-shirts, bags, mouse pads
- Theater performances
- Social media such as private or professional networks
- Information pages on the intranet or on a website
- Organizational internal media
- Public relations

---

[3] Please note that confidential content may not be published. Often, the corresponding approvals must be obtained in advance.

Minutes

Project name	*<Name of project>*	Project no.	*<Number of project>*
Location	*<Location of meeting>*	Date	*<Day.Month.Year>*
Minute taker	*<Name of minute taker>*	Version	*<0.1>*
Topic	*<Topic of meeting>*		

Attendees	*<Att1 Name, department, mail, phone>*
	<Att2 Name, department, mail, phone>
	…
	<Attn Name, department, mail, phone>
Distribution list	*<Dis1 Name, department, mail, phone>*
	<Dis2 Name, department, mail, phone>
	…
	<Disn Name, department, mail, phone>

No.	(A)ction item (D)ecision (I)nformation	Description	Responsible	Due date
<1>	*<A>*	*<Description of action item>*	*<Name>*	*<dd.mm.yy>*
<2>	*<D>*	*<Decision taken concerning specific topic>*	*<Name>*	*<dd.mm.yy>*
<3>	*<I>*	*<Description of topic to inform about>*	*<Name>*	*<dd.mm.yy>*

Fig. 2.10 Minutes template with hints

2.5   Documentation

"What you have in black and white, you can take home with confidence."
   Johann Wolfgang von Goethe (1749–1832) This section deals with the documentation during the course of a project. The documentation of the project results, for example in the form of a manual for developed software, is not considered.

2.5.1   Goals of Documentation

The goals of documentation are:

- Representation of the project results
  …for both the client and the project team.
- Representation of the current status of the project
  …with continuous documentation of the status of all work packages and tasks.
- Traceability and measurability
  What was decided, accepted and discussed? How much of the budget was spent on which tasks? What was achieved when and with what effort?
- Increase in quality
  When facts are documented, one deals intensively with the topic and automatically improves the quality.

Non-goals of documentation are:

- Documentation as an end in itself
  Don't document for the sake of documenting—documentation is too expensive for that. Important: As much documentation as necessary. Who actually needs which documents? Effort and benefit must be in a reasonable ratio.
- Only formal completion of documentation criteria
  Don't be content with the fact that certain documents are available. It should be noted that documentation is only a tool. You should not limit yourself to the mere existence of documents as a success criterion. The respective contents of the documents are important. It is wrong to assume that quality is available just because all documents have been created.

Project Documentation
According to DIN 69901-5, project documentation includes "the totality of all relevant documents that arise in or from a project, are used or applied, or have another reference to the project" [6].
   The project documentation includes, among other things:

- Initial situation and description of the problem

- Representation of the project course (e.g. project reports)
- Description of the applied solution approach
- Project costs
- Achieved benefits
- Project closure report

The project documentation is often stored in the (digital) project manual.

2.5.2   Reasons for Documentation

Why is the project documentation important?

- Documented decisions prevent repetitive discussions and thus provide security in the project.
- Timely documentation saves a lot of trouble. This makes it possible to avoid discussions and contradictions as to whether tasks have been set or accepted, who is responsible for what, which conditions apply, etc.
- Documentation is necessary in some projects to meet the statutory liability and/or warranty obligations. For example, in the field of tax law, there are storage obligations in the Tax Code (German: Abgabenordnung (AO)), in the field of commercial law the Commercial Code (German: Handelsgesetzbuch (HGB)) contains corresponding provisions. There are also extensive documentation and storage obligations in the field of medical device development.
- Quality management standards such as ISO 9000 ff. require documentation [9].

The project documentation is the basis for the following topics:

- Planning optimization
  - Planning optimization for the current project
    Sound actual values serve as a basis for plan adjustments and, if necessary, facilitate additional estimates for new scopes.
  - Planning optimization for follow-up projects in the company
    This increases the experience base in the organization. Actual values are the optimal planning basis for future projects.
- Learning organization
  Documentation can support the idea of a learning organization:
  - Only if we know our strengths can we further develop them.
  - Only if we recognize our weaknesses can we work on them.
  But note: The documentation of a lessons-learned workshop does not automatically mean that the measures defined there will actually be implemented and lived.

- Openness
  Generally accessible documentation provides transparency for all project participants and makes traceability easier, for example of decisions made in the project. This leads to
  - better communication within the team,
  - a better project climate (against formation of cliques) and
  - better representation to the outside.

Note: There may be restrictions on access to specific documents. For example, financial aspects should not be known to every project member. Generally, restricted access should prevent the dissemination of information to third parties. This applies, for example, to military projects, security-relevant projects or highly innovative research projects.

2.5.3   Requirements for Documentation

Requirements for documentation are:

- Everyone in the project should be able to find their way around.
- Standards should be offered or set, for example in the form of templates.
- Tasks, ideas, decisions, minutes of meetings and regular communication should be available in one place.
- A responsible person should take care of the documentation or rather the quality of the documentation.
- Company-wide specifications such as a corporate identity, style guides or the use of company-specific fonts and templates must be observed.

The project documentation should be centrally accessible. In an IT infrastructure, this can be, for example:

- Common project workspace
- Common internet or intranet appearance
- Collaboration software[4] such as content management systems or document management systems
- Social software such as wikis or blogs

---

[4]This refers to a technique that allows people to work or communicate together over computer networks.

2.5.4   Scope of Documentation

The scope of documentation depends on the size of the project. For example, if there is a project structure plan with work packages in the project, the documentation of the work packages is the basis for the documentation in the project. It includes protocols, status reports and the final documentation. At the latest by the project completion all project-relevant documents are required. Based on the expectations of the project completion report, the documents to be generated during the project are to be identified. With the help of a checklist, it can then be ensured that they are created early during the project. An example is shown in Fig. 2.11. This example could be extended with columns in which responsibilities and target date are stored. In the following, project documents are presented by way of example.

2.5.5   Project Profile

A project profile, also known as project brief, is typically a short summary of a project, a "one pager", presented on one DIN A4 page. It should contain the most important numbers, data and facts of the project and serves as an introduction to the project, for example as an information basis for the project kickoff. In addition, it can be used as a presentation or to represent the progress of the project with the most important project information. Figure 2.12 shows a project profile with hints. The corresponding template can be found in Sect. 6.1 on page 157.

No.	Document	Project area	File path	Originator / Supplier	Document status
1	Project order	Project management	Server1/Project/Project-order	Principal	Approved
2	Project profile	Project management	Server1/Project/Project-profile	Project manager	In progress
3	Project handbook	Project management	Server1/Project/Project-handbook	Project manager	In progress
4	Tender specification	Project management	Server1/Project/Specification	Project manager	Approved
5	Performance specification	Project management	Server1/Project/Specification	Supplier	Approved
6	Project plan	Project management	Server1/Project/Plan	Project manager	In progress
7	Work package status reports	Work package	Server1/Project/WP/Status	Work package responsible	In progress
8	Project status reports	Project management	Server1/Project/Status	Project manager	In progress
9	Work package minutes	Work package	Server1/Project/WP/Minutes	Work package responsible	In progress
10	Project minutes	Project office	Server1/Project/Minutes	Project office	In progress
11	Decisions	Project office	Server1/Project/Minutes	Project office	In progress
12	Acceptance protocol	Project management	Server1/Project/Acceptance	Principal	Initiated
13	Project closure report	Project management	Server1/Project/Closure	Project manager	Open

Fig. 2.11   Example of a project document overview

Project profile

Project name	*<Name of project>*		Project no.	*<Number of project>*
Principal	*<Name of principal>*			
Project manager	*<Name of project manager>*			
Version / Date	*<0.1 / Day.Month.Year>*		Status	*<initiated, in progress, done, cancelled>*

Steering committee	*<NN 1, NN 2, … , NN 7>*		
Project team	*<NN 1, NN 2, … , NN 7>*		
Stakeholder	*<Anyone who affects or is affected by the project>*		
Supplier	*<Anyone to support the project on request by order, e.g. external companies>*		
Project start	*<Day.Month.Year>*	Project end	*<Day.Month.Year>*
Objectives	*<Aim of the project ordered by priority>*		
Project scope	*<What has to be delivered by the project?>*		
Milestones	*<What are the most important milestones in the project? Project start, project end, most importand milestones in between>* *<Milestone 1> <Day.Month.Year> <Headline>*		
Terms of payment	*<When will which payments be made?>*		

_____   _____   _____
Place, date   Principal   Project manager

Fig. 2.12 Template project profile with hints

2.5.6 Project Manual

A project manual is useful for large projects. It contains basic project information such as contacts and project organization. In addition, it describes processes and organizational project details and contains the results of the project planning phase. As a rule, the creation and maintenance of a project manual is the responsibility of the project office.[5] There is a regular coordination with the project manager on content, scope and time lines, for example at milestones. Nowadays, a project manual is usually stored as a digital project file, either as a complete document or structured in a directory, database or document management system.

A project manual can cover the following topics:

1. Introduction, situation, strategy
2. Short description of the project, management summary
3. Contacts, project organization and project environment
4. Task descriptions and responsibilities of project team members
5. Schedule, in particular milestones
6. Methods and tools for planning and controlling the project
7. Overview of project documentation and project filing
8. Reporting, including details of when to report, and to whom, as well as when and to what extent status meetings and reviews are conducted
9. Communication rules and where to provide information
10. Description of customer responsibilities and contributions
11. Internal procedures and policies such as quality assurance, processes, escalation, accounting, etc.
12. Tools used
13. Attachments: contact information, plans, change requests, etc.

The project handbook is to be updated continuously during the implementation phase. It should always reflect the current state of the project.

2.6 Quality

"Whoever makes a mistake and does not correct it, commits a second one."
  Confucius (probably 551–479 BC) This section deals with the topic of quality in projects. At the end of the section, you will know the background and possibilities to increase the quality in your projects.

---

[5] The role of the project office is explained on page 96.

2.6.1   Quality Objectives

The goal is to ensure the quality in the project (management) itself.

Quality in Project Management
In the sense of quality management (QM), quality is the result of a comparison between quality requirements and actual condition of a unit under the aspect of a claim class. The focus in project quality management is the quality of the professional project contents. It ensures that the work results correspond to the project goals.
  The main tasks are:

- Check and ensure that a project meets the corresponding specifications
- Apply defined methods and check and ensure standards in the project
- Test the work results

The PMBOK Guide [18] lists three processes under project quality management:

- Quality planning
- Quality assurance
- Quality control

2.6.2   Procedure in Quality Management

How can quality be ensured?

- Defining a quality management role
  This role defines quality processes based on quality requirements, communicates these, checks compliance and initiates measures if necessary. The quality manager is responsible for creating and maintaining the quality manual.
- Development of a learning organization
  A learning organization has the goal of constantly developing further in order to achieve higher quality.
  - Quality from the inside out
    Quality requirements are then met when they come from the project team and, in particular, from the project management. The more important that quality is in the company's corporate identity, the higher the quality standard will be experienced in the project.
  - Generate quality, don't control it

– Understand quality in the sense of "paying attention to what is important", not in the sense of "fulfilling formalities"
– In terms of a quality guideline, always consider the ratio of effort to benefit

- Dealing with problems
  The Gemba principle[6] (Japanese for "place of action") recommends addressing problems directly where they occur. The assumption is that problems can best be understood and appropriate solutions developed directly on site. The procedure can be summarized simply:
  1. What should happen?
  2. What actually happens?
  3. Explain!

- Continuous improvement
  The idea is to introduce and support a continuous improvement process (CIP). The PDCA cycle according to Deming [5] has proven itself:
  – Plan—Developing measures to improve quality
  – Do—Implementing the planned measures
  – Control—Checking and evaluating the measures
  – Act—Initiating corrective measures as needed
    This can be achieved in projects, for example, with daily status meetings (see Sect. 3.3.5), regular retrospectives (see Sect. 4.2.6) or Lessons Learned (see Sect. 3.4.3).

- Consolidation with project partners
  Involving project partners in the presentation of work results, requests for feedback on created documents, etc. increases quality.

- Reviews
  Reviews have proven to be an efficient quality measure. These should be carried out regularly, especially at phase transitions and milestones.
  Reviews are useful for the entire project, subprojects, work packages and individual work results. Recipients of work results should be involved in reviews whenever possible. There are different variants such as informal review, technical review, walkthrough and inspection [12]. It is recommended to make reviews as simple and understandable as possible according to the KISS principle: **Keep it** short and simple.

- Use of checklists
  Checklists are one of the simplest and most successful means of quality improvement. But they must be "good" checklists. Criteria for this are that they have already proven themselves effective, are constantly updated, well formulated and have an appropriate level.

- Quality guideline, synonym *project quality plan*
  A quality guideline developed as part of the project defines quality assurance measures within the project and builds on best practices [1] as well as proven methods agreed upon within the project. This provides all project participants with a resource to draw upon and use practical quality methods within the project. Contents can include:
  – Quality processes

---

[6]Also known as the Genba principle

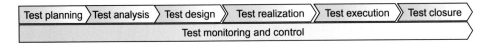

Fig. 2.13 Test activities in a test process

Which quality assurance measures apply? Here it is recommended to use general or organization-specific quality guidelines. If products are generated within the project, a test process should be defined.

In the software environment, it is recommended to take into account test activities according to the International Software Testing Qualification Board (ISTQB), as shown in Fig. 2.13 [12].

– Input and output criteria for project phases

Milestones should contain measurable criteria (see the milestone definition on page 88). These not only provide a better understanding of the expected results, but also enable targeted work within the project. The milestone deadlines are used to check the criteria and, if necessary, document any follow-up work.

– Benefits and expanding a project glossary
– Use of uniform formats

• Transparency

Regular reports should be made on the project status, preferably based on defined measurement criteria and key figures. By analyzing these reports, it can be determined early on whether project goals are at risk. In the software testing environment, these include, for example, test coverage (how many test cases have been carried out with what result), and the defect situation (how many open and closed defects there are).

• Observe company-specific conventions and regulations

It is particularly important to know them early on. This can, for example, be done as part of the contract clarification (Sect. 3.1.6). If they are not relevant, this should be documented accordingly.

• Audits

A look from the outside can be of great help. An audit includes:

– Analysis and evaluation of the project and project progress
– Discussion of problems
– Development and implementation of solutions

• Professional project management with coaching
• Qualification

This includes project manager and organizational training, each with certification, see also Sect. 5.1.

2.6.3 Checklist

Figure 2.14 shows a checklist concerning quality in the project.

Checklist quality

Question	Result
1. Is the role quality management in the project defined and assigned?	
2. Is there a quality guideline defining project standards and processes?	
3. Is there a relationship to corporate or general guidelines like ISO 9000? Are there project specific differences, exceptions or additions?	
4. Are the standards and processes on hand, before the corresponding activities start?	
5. Are all team members familiar with the standards, processes and corresponding tools in the project? Are there training courses?	
6. Is every team member instructed to follow defined standards and processes?	
7. Is the team involved in further development and adaption of the standards and processes?	
8. How is the compliance with standards and processes monitored?	
9. Is a test process defined? Is a test plan available?	
10. How is it ensured that delivered working results meet the corresponding requirements?	
11. How is the handling of quality problems? How is the handling of measures to solve them?	
12. Which criteria are defined to measure the level of the quality achieved and to serve as a basis for continuous improvements?	
13. Are project data analyzed in form of key figures, so that it is possible to early detect, when (sub) goals could not be achieved?	
14. Are there meetings concerning quality improvements between the project team and quality management?	
15. How is it checked whether or not quality improvement measures have an effect?	
16. How is the quality of resulting products ensured?	
a. Are there guidelines how to evaluate the quality of a product?	
b. Are postulated quality characteristics defined?	
c. Which measures ensure the quality of the product?	
d. How is the quality of third-party products planned?	
e. Is prototyping planned in the product development?	
f. Are quality-ensuring measures for the product manufacture already planned during product development?	
g. Is there a review plan? Who is going to review which contents when?	
h. Are there tests planned for the overall product and individual components?	

Fig. 2.14 Checklist quality

2.7   Risk Management

"Whoever never risks anything can never fail. And never win."
Paul Mommertz (*1930) Risk management stands for the systematic approach to identifying and assessing risks and the professional handling of risks found.

2.7.1   Goals of Risk Management

The most important goal of risk management is to prevent a crisis in the project. In the original meaning of the word, a crisis is a decision-making situation. In the sense of "intensification", unplanned crises are to be considered when, for example, a risk occurs. The aim is to cope with such crises, for example with fall-back solutions or a "Plan B" [1]. Here, several variants can be worked out and summarized in a decision template. It is important to actively address crises and work on them offensively. Risk management can begin with project scenarios based on the environmental analysis (see Sect. 3.1.3) with consideration of

- target scenarios;
- the best case and;
- the worst case.

These scenarios are examined in detail, measures are taken to meet identified risks and, if necessary, alternative project plans are created. Another goal is to control the risks with measures to:

- reduce the probability of risks occurring; or
- reduce the impact of risks.

> **Risk Management**
> DIN 69901-5 describes risk management as the "elimination, avoidance or reduction of project risks" [6]. Risk management is the part of project management that deals with the identification, analysis and control of risks for the planned project implementation [1]. The scope of risk management includes:
>
> - identifying risks,
> - assessing risks and
> - implementing risk mitigation measures.

2.7.2   Procedure in Risk Management

The unknown risks are critical. Therefore, every project member should be able to report risks easily and comfortably, and also be motivated to do so. Risk management should be kept simple and understandable in principle. Risk management should begin as early as possible. It is important to regularly review risks in the project, for example as part of project meetings. Here it is recommended to ask at the end: "Which risks do we still have to consider?" Below is a possible approach to risk management.

The first step is risk analysis.
Each identified risk is considered and quantified. The assessment of a risk is calculated from the probability of occurrence W multiplied by the estimated impact S. Suggestion for the quantification of risks:

- Probability of occurrence W
  - Low $= 1$
  - Medium $= 2$
  - High $= 3$
- Extent of estimated impact S
  Impact on the project in the event of occurrence
  - Less critical $= 1$
  - Critical $= 2$
  - Very critical $= 3$
- Risk $=$ probability of occurrence $W \times$ estimated impact S
  This results in low risks (values 1 and 2), medium risks (values 3 and 4) and high risks (6 and 9).

An example of representing risk management in tabular form is shown in Fig. 2.15. A template for capturing risks in the form of a risk list can be found in Sect. 6.5 on page 169.

Second step is the minimization or better avoidance of risks.
Depending on the level of the respective risk, measures are defined to reduce either the probability of occurrence or by reducing the estimated impact of the risk. The avoidance of identified risks is to be strived for. Another possibility is the acceptance of risks if one consciously decides not to take any measures for certain risks. This can make sense if, for example, one only wants to focus on the risks with the highest priority.

| Id | Risk description | | | | | Quantification | | | | Mitigation |
	Risk identification	Potential cause	Contact person	Start date	Proba-bility	Esti-mated impact	Risk	Status	Measures
R001	Disease with Covid-19	Infection during a vacation	Uwe	07-04-23	1	3	3	in progress	10.04.2023 Vacation lockout. Follow the advice of the Department of Health
R002	Errors in content and formal errors in the book	Results of the reviews cannot be published due to time reasons	Daud	11-12-22	3	2	6	done	27.04.2023 Review requests sent out early. 26.07.2023 Everything included

Fig. 2.15 Example of a risk management list

Third step is risk control.

As part of the regular consideration of risks, one should check whether the measures decided have been effective and thus the occurrence of certain risks has decreased due to a lower probability of occurrence or a lower estimated impact. In addition, one should check whether new risks have arisen and whether known risks have occurred or become obsolete.

2.8   Methods

"Method is the mother of memory."
  Thomas Fuller (1608–1661) A method is a system-neutral, more or less planned procedure for achieving a goal. This section introduces you to proven methods from the project management environment. For another overview, see, for example, the collection of methods by GPM Deutsche Gesellschaft für Projektmanagment [7].

2.8.1   Brainstorming

Brainstorming belongs to the creative techniques. This method is supposed to switch off blocks in the search for new ideas and make group work more productive. The result of this method is a collection of ideas on a given question. The following rules apply:

- Quantity before quality—the more ideas, the better.
- Free flow of imagination and fantasy—even unusual ideas are very welcome.
- Completing and improving other people's ideas is allowed.
- No criticism—criticism and evaluation follow in a later phase.

 With brainstorming, it is advisable to have a moderator and a recorder. The procedure could look like this:

1. Preparation phase (initiator)
   This phase includes the following activities:
   - Temporarily define the problem to find a precise question
   - Invite participants
   - Reserve meeting room
   - Clarify roles
2. Implementation phase (participants including initiator, moderator and recorder)
   - The moderator explains the basic rules.
   - The moderator presents the problem and the current state of discussion.
   - Start of brainstorming: All participants spontaneously express ideas for solving the problem. The moderator gives impulses if necessary.
   - The recorder notes down each idea.

- The moderator ends the phase when the previously agreed time is up or she can no longer stimulate any more ideas.

Variant: card technique

Each participant writes down ideas on paper cards with the following rules:

- One idea per card
- Write large and clearly
- A maximum of three lines per card

The recorder collects the cards. Alternatively, the participants can pin their cards to a pinboard.

3. Processing phase (participants including initiator, moderator and recorder)
    - The moderator structures the noted ideas: she sorts them and summarises them in a results list.
    - The participants go through the results list again and evaluate the ideas. The following evaluations are possible:
        - Implement immediately
        - Good, but not immediately implementable
        - Current benefits not visible
    - The not immediately implementable ideas are discussed again:
        - What could we do with it anyway?
        - How can the ideas be improved so that they can be used?
4. Final phase (participants including initiator, moderator and recorder)
    - The moderator hands over the revised results list to the initiator.
    - The moderator thanks the participants, the recorder and ends the brainstorming.

Advantages

This method quickly generates a large number of ideas with little effort in preparation and implementation. It serves the purpose of group formation. With the card query, the participants can write down their thoughts without any impairments.

Disadvantages

With complex topics, the method reaches its limits. If there are a lot of ideas, there is a lot of work for the follow-up.

Application

This is the standard method for finding ideas in a group. It is suitable for less complex problems and for getting started with a topic.

2.8.2 Problem Statement Reversal

The problem statement reversal technique headstand method (synonym: *Brainstorming paradox*) is similar to brainstorming. The question is exactly reversed and negative and absurd ideas are collected. These should contain exactly the opposite of what is actually to be achieved. In a second step, the circumstances are turned upside down and a productive result comes out. Example: How do we make our project fail? Possible answers:

- Define unclear and unmeasurable goals.
- Let people work together who don't get along.

Advantages
It is a refreshing alternative to brainstorming. Participants often find it easier to find arguments why something might not work. This generates different and new ideas.

Disadvantages
The switch from destructive to constructive thoughts can be challenging.

Application
The method is well suited for identifying potential for improvement and risks.

2.8.3 Mind-Mapping

Mind-mapping is a creative technique for visually preparing a topic [2]. A mind map quickly structures thoughts, presents information in a clear way, visualizes texts and addresses different learning types. Figure 2.16 shows a mind map, with the line thickness standing for importance or intensity.

Advantages
With a mind map, you can quickly and easily develop thoughts and new ideas. The central topic is easily grasped. The method is very suitable for learning and for getting to know new topics. All you need for implementation is a sheet of paper.

Disadvantages
If you use paper, the available space is limited. If you use mind-mapping software, exchanging and further processing data can be difficult.

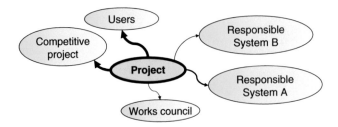

Fig. 2.16 Example of a mind map

Application

The use of mind maps is useful for individuals and small groups when written records are needed, for example:

- Working on new topics
- Preparing a presentation or written work
- Recording
- Systematic repetition of learning material

2.8.4 Method 635

The method 635 summarizes that

- 6 people
- 3 ideas write down and
- 5 times pass on (after 5 min).

It is a "brainwriting" technique that Bernd Rohrbach invented in 1968 [20]. The method helps to increase the creativity of a group.

The goal of method 635 is to find a large number of ideas and solutions for a given problem in a short amount of time. Procedure using six participants as an example:

- The problem is formulated.
- 6 participants receive a worksheet with 18 fields—3 columns and 6 rows (example in Fig. 2.17).
- In the first round, each participant writes one idea in the first line of each column, so 3 ideas.
- In a clockwise direction, this step is repeated by passing the form to the next participant five times.

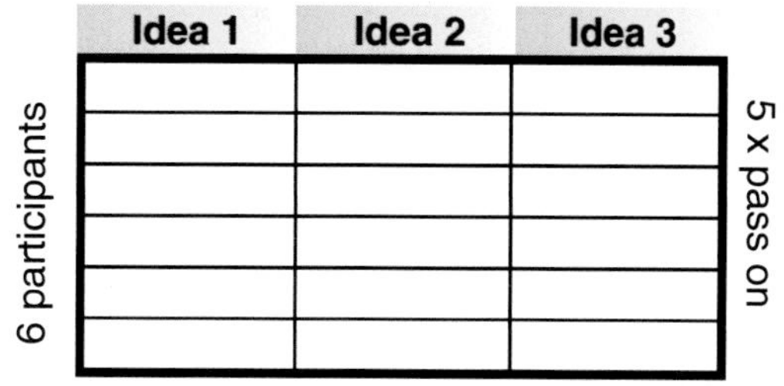

Fig. 2.17 Example of a worksheet for method 635

The following rules apply:

- The participants do not talk to each other during execution.
- The time limits must be adhered to.
- Only one idea per field.
 This procedure can also be realized with fewer participants as a variant. Then the participants work on the worksheet several times.

Advantages

This method results in many ideas in a specified time. All participants contribute, ideas are not discussed or criticized. The method can also be used if the participants are geographically distributed.

Disadvantages

The time limits can put the participants under pressure.

Application

It is suitable for small work groups and for topics of low or medium complexity.

2.8.5   Flashlight

The flashlight method is suitable for a snapshot. It can be used at any time in the project, for example:

- At a project kickoff, to query the existing knowledge about the project
- During project execution, to capture the current mood
- At the end of the project for feedback

The flashlight method can be used as follows: First, a question is asked, for example: "How well do I know the technology used in the project?" There are the statements "A lot" or "Nothing at all", but also areas in between.

- Circle
  The participants come together in a circle. One after the other, each participant says a sentence. Rule: Only one participant speaks, all others listen.
- One-point inquiry
  On a flipchart paper, the question is written at the top, and two fields are sketched below, which stand for a corresponding statement. Each participant receives an adhesive dot, which he sticks accordingly on the flipchart paper. Figure 2.18 shows an example.
- Positioning in the room

Fig. 2.18 Example of a flashlight with the one-point inquiry

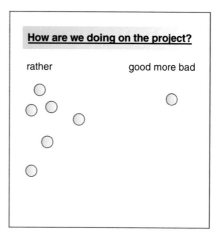

The moderator uses the free space of a room and divides it into two areas, which stand for the possible statements. The participants position themselves in theroom to answer the given question. The moderator interviews people as to whythey are standing at their position.

Advantages

It is a simple method that does not require preparation. Within a short time you get quick feedback from the group.

Disadvantages

There is a tendency to orient oneself to other group members. Therefore, it is more difficult to obtain divergent opinions.

Application

The method is suitable for quickly obtaining an impression of the mood.

2.9 Summary

The chapter "Cross-Sectional Themes" deals with all topics that are relevant across projects. These include requirements, change management, project culture, communication, documentation, quality and risk management. In addition, the chapter presents methods that have proven to be helpful in the project environment.

Requirements engineering helps to deal with requirements in order to identify product or system features for high customer benefit. In a typical project, requirements are first identified and evaluated. If these are known, the requirements are managed: they are fulfilled, fall away, change, and possibly new ones are added.

Changes are typical challenges in projects. In classical development models, a buffer for changes can be provided in simple projects. In more comprehensive projects the introduction of a change management process is recommended. In agile projects, changes are integrated into the process, so that within the planning of an iteration change requests can be considered.

The project culture describes the connectedness of the project members in the project, and the external effect of a project also plays a role. Globalization leads to international projects, in which different cultures and value systems meet each other, and this has to be considered. A common language has to be defined. The COVID-19 crisis leads to more virtual teams, increased work in the home office and use of video conferences with corresponding advantages and disadvantages. An open transparent communication between the project participants has become even more important. The project management has to concentrate on an effective project planning and control.

A key success factor for a project is good communication. Which communication means are used for a project? A communication plan shows the communication channels in the project.

Project results can be presented with the help of project documentation. Regular documentation reflects the course of the project and increases the quality of work in the project. The project manual is suitable for project documentation. A project profile shows the most important project information in a clear way.

An important aspect is quality in the project. Quality measures ensure the desired quality in the project. Good quality in the project ensures high-quality project results.

Risk management makes it possible to achieve project success even in the event of difficulties. For this purpose, the risks are collected and regularly assessed in order to take countermeasures if necessary.

Of the methods presented, brainstorming is characterized as a simple and effective method that can be used throughout the entire project life cycle. With a flashlight, a group status can be quickly obtained for a closed question.

2.10   Problems

2.1 Requirements What are the possible consequences of a non-systematic requirements analysis?

2.2 Change Management
(a) What significance and effects do changes have in classical and agile projects?
(b) Name and explain how changes can be planned and controlled in projects.

2.3 Project Culture Name some soft skills in a project.

2.4 Communication

(a) What is the effect of poor communication in a project?
(b) How can a project manager improve communication in a project?
(c) How does verbal and nonverbal communication differ?

2.5 Documentation

(a) What role does documentation play in a project?
(b) What are the quality aspects of documentation?

2.6 Quality

(a) What does quality mean to you in project management?
(b) How can quality be ensured in a project?

2.7 Risk Management

(a) Why should risk management be carried out in a project?
(b) Is risk management a one-time or an iterative process?

2.8 Methods What is a method?

References

1. Angermeier, G.: Projektmagazin Projektmanagement-Glossar (2020). https://www.projekt-magazin.de/glossarterm. Accessed: 23 Aug 2022
2. Buzan, T., Buzan, B.: The Mind Map Book: How to Use Radiant Thinking to Maximize Your-Brain's Untapped Potential. Penguin Books, New York (1996)
3. Campbell, M.: Communication Skills for Project Managers. AMACOM American Management Association (2009)
4. DeMarco, T., Lister, T.: Peopleware: Productive Projects and Teams. Dorset House, London(1987)
5. Deming, W.E.: Out of the Crisis. Massachusetts Institute of Technology, Cambridge (1982)
6. DIN Deutsches Institut für Normung e. V.: DIN 69901-5:2009-01, Projektmanagement – Projektmanagementsysteme – Teil 5: Begriffe (2009). https://www.beuth.de/en/standard/din-69901-5/113428752. Accessed: 23 Aug 2022
7. GPM Deutsche Gesellschaft für Projektmanagement e. V.: Projektmanagement an Hochschulen, Methoden (2020). https://gpm-hochschulen.de/methoden/. Accessed: 23 Aug 2022
8. IEEE Standards Board: IEEE Std 610.12-1990; IEEE Standard Glossary of Software Engineering Terminology. Tech. rep., IEEE (1990). https://standards.ieee.org/standard/610_12-1990.html. Accessed: 23 Aug 2022
9. International Organization for Standardization (ISO): ISO 9000 – Quality management (2020). https://www.iso.org/iso-9001-quality-management.html. Accessed: 23 Aug 2022
10. International Requirements Engineering Board: Lehrplan IREB Certified Professional for Requirements Engineering – Foundation Level – Version 2.2.1 (2017). https://www.ireb.org. Accessed: 23 Aug 2022

11. International Requirements Engineering Board: IREB – Home (2020). https://www.ireb.org. Accessed: 23 Aug 2022
12. International Software Testing Qualifications Board: Lehrplan Certified Tester Foundation Level, Version 2018 v3.1d (2020). https://www.german-testing-board.info/lehrplaene/istqb-certified-tester-schema/lehrplaene/. Accessed: 23 Aug 2022
13. International Software Testing Qualifications Board: Standard Glossary of Terms Used in Software Testing, Version 3.3 (2020). https://glossary.istqb.org/de/search/. Accessed: 23 Aug 2022
14. Kano, N., Seraku, N., Takahashi, F., Tsuji, S.: Attractive quality and must-be quality. J. Jap. Soc. Qual. Control **14**(2), 147–156 (1984)
15. Leffingwell, D., Widrig, D.: Managing Software Requirements: A Unified Approach. Addison-Wesley, Boston, USA (1999)
16. Mehrabian, A., Ferris, S.R.: Inference of attitude from nonverbal communication in two channels. J. Counsel. Psychol. **31**(3), 248–252 (1967)
17. Pohl, K., Rupp, C.: Basiswissen Requirements Engineering; Aus- und Weiterbildung zum Certified Professional for Requirements Engineering, 4. Aufl. dpunkt (2015)
18. Project Management Institute: A Guide to the Project Management Body of Knowledge (PMBOK Guide 6), 6th edn. Project Management Institute (2017)
19. Rajkumar, S.: Art of Communication in Project Management. Project Management Institute PMI® Research Conference: Defining the Future of Project Management; 11–14 July 2010; Washington, DC, USA. Newtown Square (2010). https://www.pmi.org/learning/library/effective-communication-better-project-management-6480. Accessed: 23 Aug 2022
20. Rohrbach, B.: Kreativ nach Regeln, Methode 635, eine neue Technik zum Lösen von Problemen. Absatzwirtschaft **12**(19), 73–76 (1969)
21. Scheffels, G., Prawitz, S.: Von der Glühlampe zur Matrix-LED (2018). https://www.automobil-industrie.vogel.de/von-der-gluehlampe-zur-matrix-led-a-712366/. Accessed: 23 Aug 2022
22. Schienmann, B.: Kontinuierliches Anforderungsmanagement, Prozesse – Techniken – Werkzeuge. Addison-Wesley (2001)
23. Siebert, H.: Der Kobra-Effekt. Wie man Irrwege der Wirtschaftspolitik vermeidet. Piper (2003)
24. Wake, B.: INVEST in Good Stories, and SMART Tasks (2003). https://xp123.com/articles/invest-in-good-stories-and-smart-tasks/. Accessed: 23 Aug 2022

Project Phases in Classical Projects

Every project has a beginning and an end, and thus a temporal course, which can be divided into project phases. At the end of this chapter, you will be able to structure and carry out your own projects based on the project phases proposed in this book, with the corresponding templates and checklists.

> **Project Phase**
> A project phase is a time period within a project. A typical separation of the phases is made by milestones, to which essential interim results are delivered for the project. Entry and exit criteria help to start and finish project phases. Every project has at least three phases:
>
> - Planning
> - Realization
> - Closure

Project management models also define project phases (see Sect. 1.3). These are structured and named differently both in the literature and within organizations. The project phases defined for this book are based on the experiences/best practice of the authors. We suggest the following phases for the implementation of your projects:

- Strategy phase (Sect. 3.1)
- Planning phase (Sect. 3.2)
- Realization phase (Sect. 3.3)
- Closure phase (Sect. 3.4)

© Springer-Verlag GmbH Germany, part of Springer Nature 2022
D. Alam and U. Gühl, *Project Management for Practice*,
https://doi.org/10.1007/978-3-662-65159-9_3

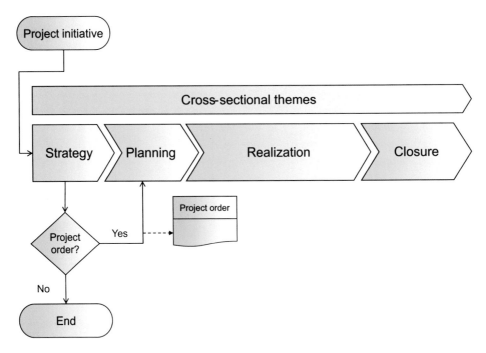

Fig. 3.1 Project phases

Figure 3.1 shows that the actual project implementation begins with the project order. However, the boundaries between the phases are not necessarily to be seen as strict, but are often also fluid—depending on the project. For example, planning can already begin while the project order is still in coordination. In some projects, a separate conceptual phase is useful, even with a division into a rough conceptual and fine conceptual phase. You can assign these to this environment of the planning phase or implementation phase. Large projects with internal and external partners usually include the creation of one or more specifications and service specifications. This is especially true for traditional industries such as automotive and machinery, energy, chemicals, logistics, real estate, construction and the public sector.

A tender is usually carried out with a tender specification. Based on this, offers follow with corresponding performance specifications. After a selection, a decision is then made on cooperation. These works are carried out in different or even in particular project phases, depending on the structure and size of the project. There is the possibility to create a tender specification even before the actual project order, so that the project order can reference it. Here it is recommended to have your own preliminary project. The creation of a tender specification can be part of the planning phase or even implementation phase.

In our experience, the topics of tender specification and performance specification are often dealt with in the strategy phase, which is why they are also dealt with in this book in the strategy phase. In the construction industry and in architectural projects, this is referred to as design planning and execution planning. More dynamic industries such as trade, media, telecommunications or information technology are increasingly moving towards agile project management (see also Sect. 5.2). Here, a framework agreement is made and the requirements and their implementation develop dynamically during the course of the project without any tender specification or performance specification.

3.1   Strategy Phase

"A strategic vision is a clear picture of what you want to achieve."
    John Naisbitt (1929-2021) Synonyms for the strategy phase include the terms *Conceptual phase, Concept phase, Project initiation* and Project preparation phase. Why do you need a strategy phase? Careful preparation avoids unnecessary risks and is the basis for a successful project execution. In the strategy phase, initial ideas are developed about how a project could be designed to achieve a defined goal, such as how a product should look at the end and how best to proceed. It is recommended to use experiences from similar projects and to rely on existing knowledge in order to avoid reinventing the wheel.

This section presents the scope of the strategy phase and provides information on what is involved in that phase of a project and what needs to be done. At the end of this section, you will have gained an understanding of what a situation analysis is and what target operationalization means, and you will be aware of the importance of a project assignment.

3.1.1   Goal and Results

The goal and result of the strategy phase is a project order. In addition, depending on the approach model, and the complexity and size of the project, other possible results include a tender specification and a performance specification.

3.1.2   Situation Analysis

"Recognizing the problem is more important than recognizing the solution, because the precise representation of the problem leads to the solution."
    Albert Einstein (1879–1955) First, the motivation for a project is to be examined. You have to inform yourself about the causes or reasons for a project and get to know the topic and the problem area. The more extensive the project, the more important it is to research, for example by studying relevant literature or searching the Internet. In addition, you can ask colleagues or experts in large companies as well as in neighboring or similar departments. You can also conduct investigations. The situation analysis should answer the following questions:

- Which information, data and facts apply?
- What opinions are there?
- Which problems are recognizable? What ideas, requirements etc. are there?
- What are the causes of the problem?
- What effects does the problem have?
- Which tasks, processes and methods are affected?
- Where are the priorities?

Try to identify the actual problem. Find out whether the issue under discussion is the actual problem or whether something deeper lies behind it. The iceberg principle often applies: Only 10 to 20% of the problem is visible, the true 80 to 90% of the cause of the problem is not mentioned.

Example: A workshop does not know where and how to store tires, which the logistics brought into the workshop. The actual problem: logistics does not care about the storage of the tires and simply delegated the problem to the workshop, whose actual task is not the storage of tires.

Find several solutions! In most cases there is more than one way to solve a problem. It is necessary to find several solutions and then identify the best one. Use the expertise of affected colleagues, other experts and the results of (literature) research. You can bring together several people and use creativity techniques to collect initial ideas (see Sects. 2.8.1, 2.8.2 or 2.8.4). Figure 3.2 shows a checklist for the situation analysis.

3.1.3   Environment Analysis

Synonyms for the environment analysis are *project environment, project context* and *stakeholder analysis*. The goal of the environment analysis is to identify all those who play or can play a role in the project and to involve them adequately. This is important because project stakeholders can decide the success of projects—positively or negatively. Therefore, it is necessary to determine stakeholders, to inform them, to support them actively and to involve them in decision-making. Why is an environment analysis necessary?

- There are different expectations and interests in a project.
  Example reorganization: consider the roles of the works council and shareholders.
  Example airport expansion: note the roles of environmental groups and the Chamber of Industry and Commerce.
- Stakeholders are affected differently, both subjectively and objectively. It is worth considering where there are synergies or conflicts.
  Example restructuring: employees with long-standing proven behavior towards new employees with new ideas.
- Different power relations

Checklist situation analysis

Project name		Project no.	
Responsible			
Version / Date		Status	

Question	Result
1. Initial situation	
a. Is the initial situation described sufficiently?	
b. Are the challenges and issues of the current situation known?	
c. Are the persons involved concerning the current situation identified?	
2. Root cause analysis	
Has a root cause analysis been executed to identify the cause of the challenges and issues of the current situation?	
3. History	
a. What activities have been carried out in the past to solve the challenges and issues?	
b. Is documentation available and why have the activities not been successful?	
c. Are experiences known concerning similar challenges and issues?	
4. Level of interests/Cooperation	
a. Has an environment analysis been conducted?	
b. Who is interested in a solution of the challenges and issues? Which group, which project supervisor, which executive?	
c. Are there projects or departments, working on the same topics?	
d. Who has interests against a project, for example competing projects?	
5. Concerning a customer / contractor situation:	
Why did the customer not solve the challenges and issues by himself?	
6. Differentiation	
a. Is it listed which activities are part of the project scope?	
b. Is it described which activities are not part of the project scope?	
c. Are there any constraints or decisions to be considered?	
7. Outlook	
a. Has a future analysis been performed for the project?	
b. Are project risks identified that could result in problems, issues and conflicts during the execution of the project?	
c. Is the impact of these risks determined?	
d. Concerning the risks and possible impact: Are best case and worst case scenarios defined including recommendations?	

Fig. 3.2   Checklist situation analysis

People in power can form opinions about the project and influence it positively or negatively.

Example: Management compared to officials in charge.

The following questions can help to identify stakeholders (see Fig. 3.3):

- Who is responsible for profit or loss through the project?
- Who are the users/customers of a developed project result?
  The development of a scenario or a vision helps here to identify who the project result will be handed over to and who will work with the project result. Who would be responsible for the operation? (see Sect. 3.4.2)
- Who is faced with the project? Who is affected?
- Are there projects that deal with similar questions?
- Which committees or working groups are to be considered?
- Who has already worked in this area?
- Are there projects that need the same resources?
- Which systems, business processes and other processes are affected?
- Are there interfaces to other projects?
- Political situation: Are there sponsors, competitors? Which executives need to be involved?

The following procedure is recommended:

- Identify stakeholders
- Determine the stakeholders' influence and attitudes towards the project
- Define measures like regular communication

To identify stakeholders, you can use mind mapping (see Sect. 2.8.3). The resulting mind map or list can be extended with contact information. Responsibilities and the ways in

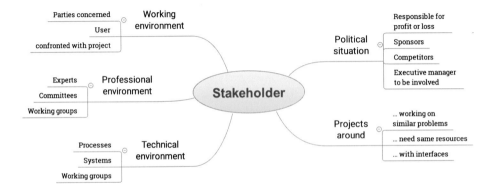

Fig. 3.3 Questions to identify stakeholders

which stakeholders are involved in the project should be defined and understood early on. This can be done, for example, using a RACI matrix. You will find a RACI matrix template in Sect. 6.8 on page 172.

RACI Matrix

A RACI matrix is used to assign roles to defined tasks.
These RACI roles in detail are:

- **R**esponsible, i.e. responsible in a disciplinary sense.
- **A**ccountable, i.e. responsible from a payer or cost center perspective.
- **C**onsulted, i.e. responsible in terms of expertise.
- **I**nformed, i.e. information needed for other responsibilities.

Figure 3.4 shows an example of an environmental analysis. A template can be found in Sect. 6.9 on page 173.

Figure 3.5 shows a checklist for the environmental analysis.

3.1.4 Project Goals

"The slowest, who does not lose sight of his goal, always goes faster than the one without a goal."

Gotthold Ephraim Lessing (1729–1781) One of the first project activities is the capture and definition of the project goal.

Stakeholder	Possible role in project	Attitude concerning project	Possible influence/ power	Measures/strategies
Director	A	positive	Very high	• Regular communication once a week
Project manager	R	positive	High	• Include in beta test phase
Customer	I	negative	High	• Regular meeting 2 times a week
User	C	negative	Low	• User workshop with demo
Works council	I	positive	Medium	• Execution of an information event

Fig. 3.4 Example for an environmental analysis

Checklist environmental analysis

Project name		Project no.	
Responsible			
Version / Date		Status	

Question	Result
1. Identification of persons / group of persons: Who is confronted with the project?	
a. Who is somehow involved in the project?	
b. Who could deliver information for the project, what sources of information are available?	
c. Are there overarching goals and visions the project should service?	
d. Are there projects under way with similar problems? Who are the contact persons?	
e. Are there other projects, requiring the same resources?	
f. What systems and processes are involved?	
g. Political situation: Are there sponsors, competitors?	
h. Who is affected by the project, who benefits, who has disadvantages?	
i. Who could influence the success of the project in a positive or negative manner?	
2. What attitude towards the project do the identified people / group of people have?	
3. How powerful are the identified people / group of people?	
4. How to deal with the identified people / group of people? How intensely should they be included into the project?	

Fig. 3.5   Checklist environmental analysis

Project Goal
DIN 69901-5 defines the project goal as "the totality of individual goals to be achieved by the project" [4].

Goals are wishes! The complete goal description is covered by answering the questions:

- What?
- How much?

- When?
- Where?

Non-goals differentiate the project and describe what the project renounces, means what should not be achieved. A strategy describes the planned path to the goal.

Project goals are necessary to steer the project and measure project success. The project goals are the basis for scope management. Based on this, the scope of the project is then defined to ensure during the course of the project that the corresponding tasks are implemented. Other reasons for objectives in the project are:

- Goals help to align and prevent detours.
- Goals serve as a basis for planning and controlling the project by "combating chance" (no surprises!)
- Goals are the basis for project control.
- Goals are motivating and community-building for the project team.
  Achieving (partial) goals is an important success factor.

Goals are thus the basis for successful projects. The following types of goals can be distinguished:

- Main goals
  These should never be lost sight of.
- Sub goals
  Sub goals help with the structuring of the project.
- Secondary goals
  Secondary goals are additional objectives that can be achieved.
- Non-goals
  In order to differentiate the project, non-goals should be stated.

The goals are to be prioritized according to their importance. It must be ensured at all times that the activities most important to the project at that time are in focus. Target operationalization helps with the precise formulation and quantification of objectives, so that success can be measured and controlled. This makes it possible to determine when a solution has been reached. The SMART method shown in Fig. 3.6 has proven itself [5]:

- **S** pecific
  The goal is formulated clearly, precisely and without contradiction formulated.
- **M** easurable
  The goal is verifiable.

Fig. 3.6 SMART-Method

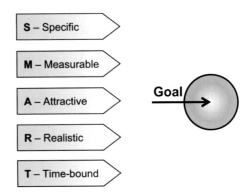

- **A** ttractive
  The goal is challenging. It challenges and is positively formulated.
- **R** ealistic
  The goal is achievable with the available resources in the available time, and framework conditions are clarified.
- **T** ime-bound
  The goal should be achieved at a certain time.

Example software test:

The developed webshop should be tested in version 2.0 on the Ubuntu 20.04 operating system with the Firefox browser in version 76.01 and the Chrome browser in version 83.0 (*specific*).

The basis for this are 400 test cases with the priority "high" and 600 test cases with the priority "medium". All test cases with the priority "high" are to be carried out completely. At least 50% of the test cases with the priority "medium" are to be carried out. At the end of the test phase, there must be no more open severe errors. Up to 10 medium-severe errors are accepted. All minor errors must be documented (*measurable*).

The tests are to be carried out according to their prioritization. Errors are to be passed on to development as quickly as possible with sufficient information for reproducibility. 20% of the test cases with the priority "high" are to be automated in parallel (*attractive*).

Ten testers are available for the project over a period of eight weeks. The basis for the planning are the tests carried out for version 1.0 with the assumption that one in ten test cases finds an error and that each error is fixed within three days (*realistic*).

The tests begin on 04.01.2021 and end on 26.02.2021, the final test report is to be created by 03.03.2021 (*terminated*).

Measurable target values describe when a target is achieved. They are therefore acceptance criteria, examples:

- 90% of all orders can be processed digitally (yes/no).
- An event has taken place (yes/no).

The target operationalization answers the following questions:

- What is to be achieved? What goals are pursued with this project?
- What is the priority of the individual goals?
- How much should be achieved? What is the target achievement?
- When should the target be achieved? What dates or periods are to be observed?
- Is there a dependency between the goals? If so, which one?
- Who is responsible for achieving which goal?
- What conditions must be met?
- Where are the goals to be achieved—what is the spatial reference?

3.1.5 Solution Approaches

"The problems that exist in the world cannot be solved with the same thought processes that created them."

Albert Einstein (1879–1955) After the goal is clear, it makes sense to think about first solutions and a schedule before submitting a project application. The solution concept is to be described. If there are several solution concepts, they are to be presented individually with their advantages and disadvantages. It should be clear how the solutions or solution approaches are prioritized. A cost-benefit analysis is recommended to show the overall benefits of a project. The economic efficiency can be demonstrated by

- quantitative (monetary) methods
  Here, the return on investment (RoI) can be calculated with the amortization time.
- qualitative (non-monetary) methods
  Here, methods such as the value analysis [12, 15] or the balanced scorecard [6] can be used.

If no economic efficiency can be demonstrated for a project or this is not desired, this should be communicated clearly. The following is a brief presentation of a possible development of solution approaches with a rough schedule using the example of a "company anniversary event":

- Planning
  - Establishing the Orga-Team (6 months before the anniversary)
  - Collecting and evaluating solution concepts: How can the anniversary be celebrated appropriately? (5 months before the anniversary)
    1. Concert with a hip-hop band
       Advantages: Unusual, even young employees are enthusiastic
       Disadvantages: Expensive, concert can go badly

2. Theater special performance
   Advantages: Culturally demanding
   Disadvantages: Not all employees like theater
3. Joint boat trip
   Advantages: Flexible number of passengers possible, community effect
   Disadvantages: Nobody can come on board the ship later or leave the ship early
   – Voting and deciding which solution concept to implement.
     (3 months before the anniversary)
* Preparing the event …
* Carrying out the event …
* Post-event follow-up …

3.1.6 Project Order

A project order is the formal starting point for the project. This makes the beginning of the project traceable.

> **Project Order**
> Synonyms: *Order, Project Manager Agreement* or *Project Agreement.* DIN 69901-5 defines the term project order as "an order to carry out a project or phase, which at least includes the following points: objectives, expected results, boundary conditions, responsibilities, planned resources, matching declaration of intent of the principle and the project responsible" [4].

With the project order, the basis for the content and scope of the project is established. The clearer you identify the requirements and wishes for the project result in the order clarification, the higher the probability of success. A clearly defined content and scope facilitates orientation in the project. Depending on the project context, the term content and scope can stand for both the project (What is to be done?) as well as for the intended project result (What is achieved by the project?). The scope management ensures that the project contains all the work tasks to successfully implement the project [10]. In the course of the project, the following advantages arise from a project order:

* The team members have an orientation
  This provides satisfaction and leads to motivation and acceptance.
* The project organization is in operation
  This results in very good coordination and a controlled process flow. Conflict management is possible.

- The project planning is complete
  A clear project mandate avoids planning errors. Any differences or problems that may arise in the project can be recognized early and allow early adaptation of the planning.

The most important points for the project mandate are to be clarified, written down and finally confirmed in writing by the principal. The scope and granularity of the project mandate depend on the size of the project. It should contain the following:

- Principal
  A project manager always needs a contact person, even if there is a body behind this, such as a steering committee, whose decisions can have an impact on the project. It should be clear who will accept the project result at the end.
- Purpose of the project
  Are the principal's ideas and wishes known?
  Description of the problem and the task: What is it about?
  Task definition: What is it not about?
- Goal
  What is achieved when the project is finished; what are the quality criteria for this?
  What are the critical success factors?
- Short project description
- Project structure and project organization
  Description of the committees, the project manager and the project members.
- Resource plan and schedule
  Resources, costs, budget, as well as dates and milestones are to be listed.
- Risks
  The currently known risks and, if possible, the first corresponding measures are to be listed (see also Sect. 2.7).

An overview of the project order is shown in Fig. 3.7, a template can be found in Sect. 6.10 on page 174. From the project order, a project profile can be derived (see Sect. 2.5.5). It is recommended to keep a project manual from this point on (see Sect. 2.5.6).

Tip: In this phase, you should try to attract top-ranking sponsors as patrons in the company and inform them regularly.

3.1.7 Tender Specification

The tender specification describes what is to be delivered. It contains the binding requirements, expectations and wishes for a planned product and includes the deliveries and services of a contractor.

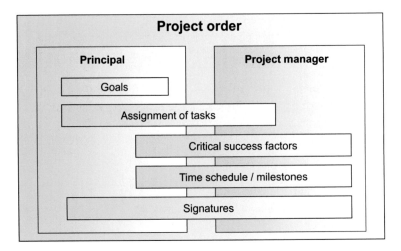

Fig. 3.7   Scope of the project assignment and involved roles

Tender Specification
Synonyms are: *Requirements catalog, requirements specification,* requirements document, *rough concept, performance list, framework document* or *system requirements*

   According to DIN 69901-5, a tender specification describes the "set of requirements specified by the principal for the deliveries and services of a contractor within a contract" [4]. A tender specifications describes the requirements, expectations and wishes for a planned product. It is often part of a contract in information technology, electrical engineering and automotive engineering.

The need for a tender specification in a project depends on several parameters. In general, the larger and more complex a project, the longer the duration and the more external partners in a customer/supplier relationship, such as system suppliers, are present in the project, the greater the need for a tender specification to be created.

   The tender specification (and later the performance specification) is primarily an important tool in the project for clear communication and good understanding of the requirements. Since the creation of tender specifications and performance specifications always involves effort, the cost-benefit ratio must be considered in each case. With a tender specification, it is ensured that all requirements are stored in one source. It is typically the basis of a project and serves at the end of the project as the basis for acceptance in order to confirm the successful implementation of the requirements. The tender specification contains the requirements based on the project order and serves as the basis for requesting proposals (call for offers) in customer/supplier projects. The principal himself should create the tender specification. If this is not possible, he must at least approve it. The tender specification should avoid a possible different interpretation of general requirements between the principal and the contractor. The following is a proposal for the contents of a tender specification:

- Project goals
- Tender documents
- Feasibility studies (concept descriptions)
- Starting situation (technical and organizational), for example functionality of legacy systems
- Requirements
  The requirements should be structured according to domain and follow standards such as ISO/IEC/IEEE 29148:2018 [8] or the quality characteristics according to ISO/IEC 25000:2014 [7]. For example, requirements in the IT sector could be structured as follows (see also Sect. 2.1):
  - Technical requirements (system performance, availability, performance, volume framework, security requirements, design criteria)
  - System requirements (functionality, interfaces, hardware, software, databases, services)
  - Infrastructure requirements (network, power, climate, space, fire protection, place of business)
  - Operational requirements (maintenance and repairs during and after the warranty period)
- Constraints (non-functional requirements, quality requirements, laws, standards, company-specific regulations, data protection, environmental protection, decommissioning)
- Operational requirements, existing and/or planned operational processes and organizational procedures such as guidelines, procedures and work instructions.
- Contracts and ongoing projects in the project environment (applicable regulations and requirements that must be observed in the project environment)
- Other conditions (transportation, customs regulations)
- Services of the contracting authority/contractor (collaboration, ancillary services)
- Communication plan, workshops/coordination with the principal
- Documentation (technical product documentation, user manual, administration and operation manual)
- Training (users, administrators, operation)
- Acceptance and commissioning

The following are tips for creating a tender specification:

- Pay attention to conflicts or contradictions between individual requirements, clarify general global customer requirements in order to obtain clear project requirements.

- Formulate the project requirements solution-neutral.
  Example: The web shop is 97% available in the year.
- Prioritize your requirements.
  - Must criteria: Requirements that must be implemented in any case.
  - Should criteria: Requirements that are to be implemented, but which may possibly be dispensed with.
  - Could criteria: Requirements that are not necessarily to be implemented.
- Use the knowledge of your project employees for the creation of the tender specification.
- Invest enough time and resources in the determination of the project requirements and in the creation of the tender specification.
- Agree on the project requirements and the tender specification with all project participants, in particular with the principal, in a binding manner.
- Carry out requirements that you have identified but which the principal does not consider relevant (e.g. data protection aspects, company guidelines) separately as "requirements not to be fulfilled" for your own protection.

In project practice, it has been shown that there can also be improvements or changes to completed tender specifications. This topic must be taken seriously and changes are to be regulated with a change management process (see Sect. 2.2). For example, it must be ensured that everyone who works with the tender specification is always involved in changes and has access to the latest version.

3.1.8   Performance Specification

The performance specification describes how a service is to be provided. It contains the implementation guidelines which are to be developed by the contractor. The specification thus describes the planned implementation of the tender specification provided by the principal.

Performance Specification
Synonyms are: *Execution planning, detailed design concept, technical specification, fine concept, functional specification, project specification, ideal concept,* or *feature specification.*
   The performance specification according to DIN 69901-5 includes the "realization plans developed by the contractor on the basis of the tender specification handed over by the principal" [4]. It thus represents the concretization of the tender specification. The performance specification is the contractually binding, detailed description of a service to be provided.

Fig. 3.8 Tender
specification as basis for
performance specifications

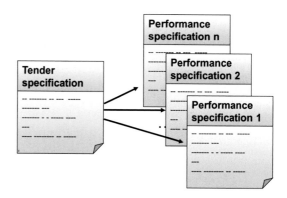

The basis for the performance specification is the tender specification: without a tender specification there can be no performance specification. As displayed in Fig. 3.8, a tender specification can be the basis for several performance specifications, for example as part of a call for tenders. Therefore, the tender specification is to be checked in detail for technical and economic feasibility and freedom from contradictions. The performance specification describes the planned implementation of the requirements from the tender specification. It includes the services required for achieving the project objectives in detail, namely technically, economically and organizationally. The realization of the project requirements and the conditions for this are agreed upon. Depending on the project, a detailed performance specification may also include a complete project plan, including time schedule and resource plan. As a binding agreement between the principal and the contractor, the performance specification is the basis for project implementation and serves as a project basis. The performance specification should be created in close coordination with the principal and signed at the end by both sides. Changes should be processed within a defined change management process. Agreed changes must be made in writing and countersigned (see Sect. 2.2).

3.1.9   Checklist

Figure 3.9 shows a checklist for the strategy phase.

3.2   Planning Phase

"Planning replaces chance with error."
  Albert Einstein (1879–1955) The planning phase lays the foundation for a successful project. A project plan shows how the project mandate issued in the strategy phase can be implemented in concrete terms. In addition to project implementation, project planning is the central task of the project manager. A project is divided and structured in order to reduce complexity and to gain and maintain an overview. It must be noted that the goal always remains in focus. The goal is more important than the plan.

Checklist strategy phase

Project name		Project no.	
Responsible			
Version / Date		Status	

Question	Result
1. Project order	
a. Has a project order been placed?	
b. Who is the principal?	
c. Are the project goals agreed upon?	
d. Are the project goals measurable?	
e. Are conditions defined?	
f. Are the non-goals of the project defined?	
g. Who will be the project manager?	
h. Are the known risks listed?	
2. Has a situation analysis been executed?	
3. Has an environmental analysis been conducted?	
4. Initial planning activities	
a. Are drafts available concerning project structure and project organization?	
b. Are there estimates concerning required resources?	
c. Is there a rough time schedule with milestones?	
d. Is a first communication plan prepared?	
e. Are there ideas concerning the set-up of a project team?	
5. Profitability analysis	
a. Has a profitability analysis been conducted?	
b. Are in particular follow-up costs considered?	
6. Tender specification	
a. Are tender specifications required in the project?	
b. Are tender specifications available in the project?	
c. Who prepares a tender specification and by when?	
d. Who approves a tender specification and by when?	
7. Performance specification	
a. Are performance specifications required in the project?	
b. Are performance specifications available in the project?	
c. Who prepares a performance specification and by when?	
d. Who approves a performance specification and by when?	

Fig. 3.9   Strategy phase checklist

No plan can map reality 100% and thus planning is always a balancing act. On the one hand there is the theory: The better a project is planned, the more likely the project will be successful. On the other hand, there is the danger of bureaucratic over-planning: Planning becomes a substitute for project work—so much planning that one does not get to the actual project.

It must be clear to all project participants that a plan can only be an approximation. A presented plan, even in an interim version, facilitates communication, especially with the people to be involved. In addition, coordination is easier, for example when requesting resources required. Planning also provides the opportunity to identify possible problem areas at an early stage and to address them specifically. In general, and also for project planning, the following applies: The earlier a mistake is recognized, the lower the costs of rectification. Alternative scenarios can be thought through and taken into account in the planning. At the end of the planning phase there is a coordinated plan. In a kickoff meeting, the project team should say: "This is how it could work". Then the actual project implementation begins.

A plan lives! First, it is a rough framework that is gradually developed and coordinated. In the end, there is a coordinated state. But even after the planning phase is completed, the plan must be checked regularly and adapted to actual conditions. This section introduces you to activities in the planning phase and provides you with information on what to consider in the planning phase of a project. At the end of this section, you can create a project plan that includes a work breakdown structure, a cost and resource plan, a time schedule with milestones, and a project organization. You understand how to create, optimize, and coordinate these plans. You are aware of the importance of holding a suitable project kickoff event, depending on the type and size of the project.

3.2.1   Objectives and Results

The objectives and results of the planning phase are

- a complete project plan including a work breakdown structure, time schedule, resource and cost plan, and project organization, and
- a successfully completed project kickoff event.

3.2.2   Project Plan

"Nobody plans to fail, but most fail to plan."
   Lee Iacocca (1924–2019) What is a project plan?

Project Plan
According to DIN 69901-5, the project plan is the "collection of all plans available in the project" [4]. The project plan includes all plans that are created in the project, usually these are

- Work breakdown structure (see Sect. 3.2.3),
- Time schedule including milestone plan (see Sect. 3.2.4),
- Resource and cost plan (see Sect. 3.2.5).

Even if project planning is along with project controlling the central task of a project manager, you should always be aware that project management is the achievement of objectives, not the fulfillment of plans!

Example: In a project "Exam Preparation" there is the following planning:

1. Learning the lecture notes
2. Learning the homework
3. Working through existing exam tasks
4. (For oral exams) "Playing through" exam situations

Even with optimal planning, the exam is not passed yet. The project "Exam Preparation" is only really successful with the successful completion of the exam, i.e. the achievement of goals.

A plan is a guideline. It is never exact and becomes outdated as soon as it is finished. Even a wrong plan is better than no plan at all, but please keep in mind: There are limits to planability. Do not adjust the project to the plan. The project plan answers the following questions:

- What?
  Identify and describe the subprojects, work packages and tasks; The result is the work breakdown structure.
- Until when?
  Describe the timeline; The result is the time schedule and milestone plan.
- Who/how many?
  Show which forces are to be used with which qualification, which personnel and material resources are needed. This is documented in the resource and cost plan. The project organization describes the type of cooperation.
- Conditions?
  Specify the technical and spatial requirements, list the known restrictions. This is noted directly in the project plan.

One of the biggest challenges of project planning is the balanced consideration of the following three aspects:

- *Quality*
  Project scope that should be achieved with a defined quality
- *Costs*
  Effort in form of resources to be used
- *Time*
  Deadline, when the project has to be finished

It is called a magical triangle (see Fig. 3.10), because the change of one size influences the other or both other sizes [1].

Example: After planning, the project duration is fixed to develop a product ready for series production. To shorten the project duration now, either the scope of functions must be reduced or the team must be enlarged.

As already mentioned in Sect. 2.3.3 we work with people in the project. Good communication with all stakeholders (i.e. the exchange of information), is part of good planning. Communication is a prerequisite for the formation of project teams and enables goal-oriented cooperation (see also Sect. 2.4). Try to identify the interests of your principal from the beginning and include them in any further project planning. Integrate the future project members into your planning. This not only makes the planning more secure, but also leads to increased motivation of the participants. Consider the personal goals and expectations. Do the people identify with the project? Do the participants even have time? Involve superiors in case of time conflicts.

Expect changes. As mentioned in Sects. 2.1 and 2.2 there is a smaller or larger scope of changes to requirements in practically every project. These should be processed as part of a change management process. Suggestion: Try to consider a buffer for requirements changes during planning, especially in larger projects. This simplifies change

Fig. 3.10 Magical triangle of projekt management

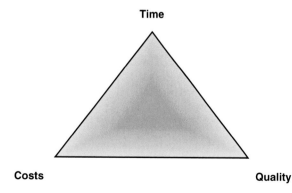

management and reduces the risk of time and cost overruns with subsequent necessary extra orders and budget increases. The following order results in the planning phase:

- Create a work breakdown structure together with likely project members (Sect. 3.2.3)
- Carry out time scheduling with determination of milestones (Sect. 3.2.4)
- Plan resources and costs (Sect. 3.2.5)
- Determine project organization(Sect. 3.2.6)
- Carry out optimizations (Sect. 3.2.7)
- Coordinate the project plan with the principal (Sect. 3.2.8)

At the end of the planning phase, the project kickoff stands; this needs to be prepared, carried out and followed up. All project employees need orientation. Therefore, communicate the project plan well. Make it easily accessible and visualise it, for example with a poster.

3.2.3   Work Breakdown Structure

What is a work breakdown structure?

Work Breakdown Structure (WBS). The WBS is part of the project plan. According to DIN 69901-5, the WBS is the "complete hierarchical representation of all elements (subprojects, work packages) of the project structure as a diagram or list" [4]. The representation or structure can be carried out in the following ways:

- functionally,
- object-oriented,
- task-/process-oriented,
- mixed-oriented.

The WBS subdivides the project into planned and controllable

- subprojects
  There is a regional, organizational or subject-related division.
- work packages
  It is a self-contained task. If necessary, there are additional levels such as main work package and/or sub-work package.
- tasks
  Tasks are typically listed in work packages.

Why and for what purpose do you need a work breakdown structure?

The work breakdown structure is a basis for:

- distributing responsibilities in the project,
- estimating the time required and the project costs,
- controlling the project and
- having a basis for project documentation.

What does a work breakdown structure consist of?

In order to be able to record a project as simply, completely and clearly as possible, project structuring is required, comprising all necessary activities in order to achieve the project goal.

Requirements for project structuring include clearly defined project goals and project requirements. The result of planning a project structure is the work breakdown structure. The WBS provides an overview of the entire project by hierarchically structuring it. Starting from the project at the top level via an intermediate level with subprojects, the lowest level finally results in the work packages (cf. Fig. 3.11):

- Project
  The project is the highest term, it is derived from the project order and the project goal formulated therein.
- Subprojects
  The project is divided into subprojects according to certain criteria, possibly with project managers for the technical control.
- Work packages
  Work packages are usually not further subdivided. As a rule, one person works on a work package. But, for instance, in research projects often several people work on a work package. If work packages are too large, additional divisions are possible, for example:

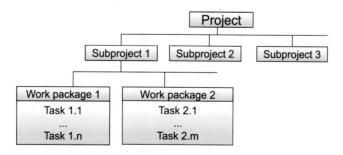

Fig. 3.11   Elements of the work breakdown structure (WBS)

- – Main work package,
- – Work package,
- – Sub-work package.
- Tasks
  Depending on the granularity and dynamics of the project, the tasks in the project are defined within the work packages. The tasks are listed as content in the work packages, for example in work package descriptions, and are thus the smallest units of the project. They are the "atoms (elementary particles)" of a project.

The quality of the WBS depends on the complete description of all project-relevant objects and/or activities and, in particular, the resulting work packages. What do you need to know about the work packages?

Work packages are the lowest objects in the work breakdown structure. They should be clear and verifiable, without contradictions and overlaps with other work packages. The temporal sequence of work packages does not play a role yet. Therefore, avoid discussions about the temporal sequence when structuring the project.

The goal for work packages is to assign costs, resources and time expenditure as unambiguously as possible. The scope of the work packages can be very different: from a simple completed task (design specification) to a complete development order (developing a web shop). For better project overview and representation of relationships, a similar granularity of work packages is recommended. Work packages which are too large make it difficult to keep track of the project progress. Work packages which are too small lead to high administrative effort. A work package includes:

- Naming of the responsible person and, if applicable, the processor
  A deputy should also be listed here.
- Task description
  Detailed description of the task, the services to be provided and the expected work results.
- Acceptance criteria
  When is the work package satisfactorily processed? Acceptance criteria are to be defined by the person who receives the work result.
- Processing effort
  Includes the estimated time required (best estimated by the processor himself).
- Resource requirements
  This includes the personnel to be used, material requirements and, if necessary, external services and expected costs.
- (Optional) Unique number in WBS
  A numbering system is particularly useful in large projects in order to improve and unambiguous assignment.
- (Optional) Interfaces to other work packages

In order to optimize cooperation in the project, to avoid frictional losses and to clarify dependencies, the relationships to other work packages should be listed.
- (Optional) Quality assurance measures
- (Optional) Risks
  Note: It should be considered whether risks identified in work packages are better processed centrally in project risk management.

How do I structure a work breakdown structure?

The project structuring can be carried out according to different criteria; accordingly, different WBS structures are possible:

- Function-oriented WBS
  This results in a structuring according to activities, which makes it easier to assign to functional areas. This is suitable for service projects such as a company party or cultural event. Figure 3.12 shows an example.
- Object-oriented WBS
  Here all relevant objects or parts of the project are listed, such as hardware, software, documents, etc. This is illustrated as an example in Fig. 3.13. For products, the result is an overview of the individual components and parts in the form of a bill of material (BoM).
- Process-oriented WBS
  The representation follows a chronological order, for example in a development process with the steps analysis, design and implementation. Figure 3.14 shows an example.

Fig. 3.12   Example of a function-oriented WBS

Fig. 3.13   Example of an object-oriented WBS

Fig. 3.14   Example of a process-oriented WBS

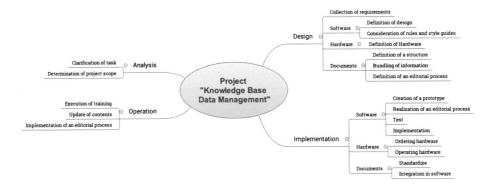

Fig. 3.15   Example of a mixed-oriented WBS

- Mixed-oriented WBS
  Often a pure object- or function-oriented structure cannot be created, so in practice mixed structures often arise. In Fig. 3.15 the structuring was done in the first level according to processes (process-oriented), in the second level partly according to objects (object-oriented).

What can I do with the finished work breakdown structure?
  Depending on the size and complexity of the project, the following outcomes will result:

- Time schedule (see Sect. 3.2.4)
  This includes the time planning and milestones.
- Resource and cost plan (see Sect. 3.2.5)
  This includes personnel and material costs as well as the required budget. This is used to estimate the costs.
- Staff requirements (see page 92)
  Depending on the project, different expertise is required, which should be completely mapped in the project.

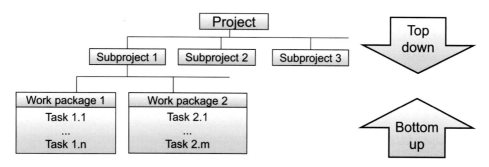

Fig. 3.16   Top down and bottom up

- Risk analysis
  From the work packages, specific risks can be derived (see Sect. 2.7).
- Planned documentation and communication in the project.

How do I create a work breakdown structure?
There are two main approaches to creating a work breakdown structure (Fig. 3.16):

- Top down—deductive approach—from the general to the individual
  Starting from the project goal, subprojects and finally work packages are created.
  Useful for clear projects.
- Bottom up—inductive approach—from the individual to the general
  First, the work packages for the project goal are collected, in the next step the work packages are grouped into subprojects.
  Recommended for complex projects.

A mixed form is also conceivable. For example, a project manager could structure the project top down and ask her team to independently define work packages. She then checks both results and brings them together.
The following are additional tips for work breakdown structures :

- Reuse existing work breakdown structures
  Check if you can rely on work breakdown structures from similar projects.
- Create the work breakdown structure as a team
  As a basic project planning activity, it is best to create the WBS together with the entire project team or, in the case of larger projects, with the core team.
  As a method, a joint structuring with Metaplan wall and moderation cards offers a good overview for everyone. Furthermore, assignments can be changed quickly and flexibly.
- Use external expertise
  If necessary, call on (project) external specialist knowledge for project structuring.

- Work with pictures and graphics
  Visualize the WBS created together in a prominent place so that you and your team have an overview of the project.
- Consider effort for project completion
  Often, project results are handed over as part of the final project activities. This effort should not be underestimated and should be taken into account in the planning (cf. Sect. 3.4).
- Regularly check the work breakdown structure
  It is important that the WBS remains up-to-date over the entire project duration.
- Use the work breakdown structure to measure project progress
  There is project management software in which you can record the WBS and document progress in the project when, for example, work packages are completed. This results in an up-to-date picture of the project status at regular intervals. Examples include MS Project [9], Jira [2] and ProjectLibre [11].

Figure 3.17 shows a checklist for the work breakdown structure.

3.2.4   Time Schedule

The time schedule arranges the work packages identified in the work breakdown structure into a realistic project sequence.

> **Time Schedule**
> Synonym: *Timetable*.
>   The time schedule is part of the project plan (Sect. 3.2.2) and shows the timeline of the project with start, end and milestones. It shows the duration of the individual work packages within a project graphically, for example in the form of bar charts or flowcharts.

The following procedure is possible:

- Determination of the sequence of work packages
  The work packages are brought into a temporal sequence.
- Temporal arrangement of work packages
  After consultation with the persons responsible for a work package, the project management defines a start and end date for each work package in a time schedule. The temporal arrangement depends on the duration of the work packages, buffer times and resource availability as well as on the resource and cost planning.
- Determination of milestones

Checklist work breakdown structure (WBS)

Project name		Project no.	
Responsible			
Version / Date		Status	

Question	Result
1. Procedure to prepare a work breakdown structure (WBS)	
a. Is it decided what method to follow?	
Inductive (bottom up) or deductive (top down)?	
b. Were all project related tasks completely collected by people affected?	
c. Have the tasks been structured and assigned to subprojects as well as work packages (main or sub work packages)?	
d. Are responsibilities assigned?	
2. Takes the breakdown within the WBS place at the different levels (from project to subproject, from subproject to work packages) in each case into about five to ten comprehensible entities?	
3. Is there a subproject / work package „Project management"?	
4. Work packages	
a. Can work packages be assigned to team members with full responsibility?	
b. For every work package is there a responsible and a representative (pair principle)?	
c. Is there a profile of qualification with required capacities?	
d. Are the work packages described sufficiently precise with expected results and scope of work?	
e. Are not more than seven people working on a work package so that there is a manageable granularity?	
f. Is the work load of a work package at least a month (about 160 hours)?	
g. Is the duration of a work package not shorter than three months?	
h. Is the time required by individual work packages consistent with the time required by the whole project?	
i. Do the WBS and the time schedule match?	
j. Is the cost volume of the work packages in proportion to the total project costs?	
k. Do the WBS and the resource plan / cost schedule fit together?	
5. Has the WBS been coordinated with the project members?	

Fig. 3.17   Checklist for the work breakdown structure

The start and end dates are synchronized and linked with milestones.
- Planning review
  Due to temporal dependencies (e.g. a follow-up work package requires results from another work package) and temporally limited resources (e.g. expensive tools), there are conditions for the overall project schedule.

The time schedule can be created from the project start or from the project end in a forward calculation or in a backward calculation.

The work packages whose start and end dates cannot be moved result in the critical path. If processing times of work packages in the critical path change, this has a direct effect on the total project duration. Figure 3.18 shows an example for this.

This results in a minimum duration of $2 + 7 + 3 + 9 = 21$ days.

Milestone/Milestone Plan
Synonyms: *Release, Customer release,*
    Stop-or-Go Point, Quality Gate, or *Review Point.*
    According to DIN 69900, a milestone is an "event of special importance" [3]. This is the realization of intermediate goals with an important project result. Milestones are a key component of project management, especially project controlling, and often define phase transitions. A milestone includes

- a date and
- expected results with verifiable criteria.

The contents of a milestone plan are

- project start date
- milestone dates
- project end date

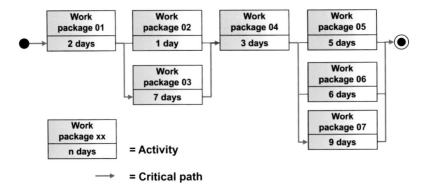

Fig. 3.18   Example for a critical path

Milestones are aligned with important events such as go-live dates, trade fair dates or steering group meetings. They summarize the end dates of one or more work packages, which results in a phase plan. This should be created in agreement with the principal. Activities from the WBS then run together in the milestones. In addition to the acceptance criteria for the work packages, specific quality criteria for the acceptance of the milestones can then be defined.

The number of milestones should be defined according to the size and length of the project. In practice, a maximum of eight to ten milestones has proven to be effective. Figure 3.19 shows an example of a milestone plan.

In general, the following steps apply to each milestone:

- Planning
- Execution
- Review
- Closure

This specifically means for milestone planning:

- The next milestone must be planned in detail in terms of content.
- The milestone after next is to be planned in terms of time and at the level of headings.
- The overall plan is to be adapted and updated
  Conflicts in terms of time and scope of milestones are to be identified and clarified here.

The following methods can be used as planning techniques:

- Bar chart (see Fig. 3.20)
- Network planning technique with forward or backward calculation
- Milestone planning

Figure 3.21 shows a checklist for the time schedule.

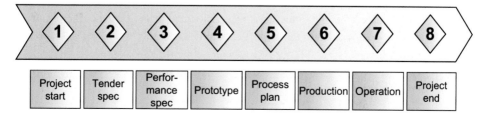

Fig. 3.19   Example of a milestone plan

Fig. 3.20 Example for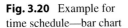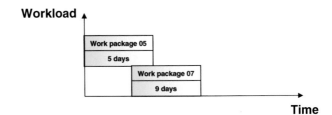
time schedule—bar chart

3.2.5   Resource and Cost Plan

Resource Plan
The resource plan is part of the project plan and describes which human and material resources are required to implement the project.

Typically, the most important resource in projects is the personnel deployed. As a result, the majority of resource planning is personnel planning. Sometimes resource planning is the same as personnel planning, in which case it is referred to as a human resources plan (synonyms: *human resources estimation personnel deployment plan*). This is based on the effort required for each work package in the work breakdown structure.

Cost Plan
The cost plan is part of the project plan. According to DIN 69901-5, the cost plan is the "presentation of the costs incurred for the project, which may also include the cost curve" [4].

The project and of course the project employees need resources. Resource planning estimates and plans the resource requirements. Since a budget is required for the resources, resource planning is usually done in parallel with cost planning. The goal of resource and cost planning is to calculate the total project costs. In particular, in matrix project organization (see Sect. 3.2.6), it should be clarified with the resource planning, as to which resources can be made available to the line organization and to what extent. The resources in the company and especially in the project should be optimally utilized. The following must be distinguished:

- Material resources
  This includes suitable premises, machines, tools, IT infrastructure, office equipment, tools—for example development environments, test tools, etc.

Checklist time schedule

Project name		Project no.	
Responsible			
Version / Date		Status	

Question	Result
1. Is there a work breakdown structure (WBS) as a basis for the time schedule?	
2. Milestones	
a. Does the number of milestones fit the size and duration of the project?	
b. Is the next milestone planned in detail, coordinated, and decided?	
c. Is there a fixed date for the next milestone?	
d. Is the next but one milestone defined regarding heading level and date?	
3. Are influences by other projects considered in the time schedule?	
Was there a corresponding coordination with other projects?	
4. Is the critical path defined concerning dependencies and duration?	
5. Completeness of the time schedule	
a. Were further education and training periods taken into account?	
b. Were holidays, holiday seasons, sick leave, and absentee time considered?	
c. Are additional time buffers included?	
6. Is the time schedule consistent in the project?	
Does the sum of times of the working packages fit the overall schedule?	
7. Has the time schedule been coordinated and reviewed by the project team?	

Fig. 3.21 Time Schedule checklist

- Human resources
  Costs are incurred for the project manager and each participating person in the project. Different skills with different costs, external or internal expert, resource bottlenecks, time and space availability must be considered here. Depending on the type of project and the size of the project, there may be a separate personnel resource plan.
- Other costs
  Costs that cannot be assigned to material or human resources; e.g. travel expenses, expenses for project advertising material, etc.

In practice, the cost estimation for a project is based on the WBS and the work packages listed there. Each work package provides corresponding plan numbers, which are added together for the subprojects. Finally, the cost estimation is made for the entire project.

The key here is the quality of the schedule data reported by the work packages; these should be checked and, if necessary, critically questioned: Have employee absences (vacation, illness, training) been taken into account? Have communication costs for meetings and workshops been calculated? Has a need for qualification and familiarization been planned? Have quality measures such as reviews and training been taken into account?

In addition, there are the following methods for cost or effort estimation:

- Simple estimation with estimation packages
- Cost estimation according to phases with personnel or material costs
- Expert estimation
  The Delphi method has proven itself effective [13]. Here, in a multi-stage process, several experts are consulted. Each expert estimates the effort for work packages independently of others. Then the results are combined. If there are large differences, explanations for the deviations are collected and the experts review their estimates. The goal is to achieve consensus within a tolerance range.
- Comparison with similar projects
- Algorithmic cost model
  As an example, the Constructive Cost Model (COCOMO) by Barry Boehm for IT projects [14]. This is an algorithmic model. With the help of company-specific parameters such as code lines to be delivered and the complexity of the project, the number of person-months and the duration of the project are estimated.

Risk surcharges must be taken into account in the estimates. The conduct of cost estimation workshops has proven itself. The personnel resource plan is usually based on the costs of each work package in the work breakdown structure. These are estimated in steps, for example:

1. Estimating the amount of work
   This requires experience from similar or previous projects, the employee is to be involved.

Example: The affected employee estimates 10 person days of effort.

2. Estimating the extent to which an employee can work on the project.

Example: Due to other commitments, the employee can work on the project 25% of their availability.

3. The actual total requirement results from division of the amount of work by the work intensity.

Example: The result is (10 days/25% =) 40 days total duration.

4. Adjusting the total duration

If the work can be divided up well, a simple adjustment of the total duration is possible by the number of project employees available at the same time.

However tasks are not divisible at will.

Example: Without taking into account an increased training effort, additional communication needs, etc., this results in a total duration of 20 days for 2 project employees (40 days/2 =).

A procedure for personnel planning is:

- Determining the personnel requirements
- Determining the available capacity
- Comparison of capacity and demand
- Capacity balancing or capacity, schedule and cost optimization

Figure 3.22 shows a checklist for resource and cost planning.

3.2.6 Project Organization

Project Organization

DIN 69901-5 describes the project organization as the "structural and procedural organization for the implementation of a specific project". The project organization can consist of parts of the existing corporate organization and is then supplemented only by project-specific regulations [4]. Possible organizational forms (the most common are **bold** highlighted) are:

- Pure functional project organization (by areas, departments)
- **Functional project organization**
  Synonyms are: *Influence Project Management Project Coordination, Line Project Organization* or *Staff Project Organization.*
- **Matrix Project Organization**
  The synonym *Matrix Project Management* is also known.

- **Pure Project Organization**
  Synonyms for this are *Pure Project Management* or *Taskforce*.
- Project society

The project organization includes:

- Roles such as principal, project manager, controller, etc.
- Committees such as Steering Committee, Core Team, Project Team, Extended Project Team or Working Groups.
- Organizational regulations such as a project manual.
- Project organization chart showing the reporting and decision-making process.

The above-mentioned forms of project organization are characterized as follows:

- Pure functional project organization
  Here the project management has relatively little importance. The project is carried out in a given organizational structure, but line work takes precedence. The advantage is better access to the project employees. The risk is that the given hierarchy with its strengths and weaknesses is maintained.
- Functional project organization
  In this organizational form, the project employees remain in the line organization. The project manager does not have direct access to the project team, but advises and mediates between the departments involved. Since she or he reports directly to the management, she or he still has a great deal of influence on the project.
- Matrix project organization
  This is a hybrid form between a pure project organization and project coordination. Responsibility and authority are divided between the project manager and the involved line functions. Project employees are responsible for a certain share in the project, but remain anchored in the line organization at least personnel-wise. The possible better coping with fluctuations in utilization is advantageous. However, risks include possible conflicts due to unclear responsibilities in double subordination or contradictory requirements from line and project organization.
- Pure project organization
  For the duration of the project, the employees involved are fully assigned to an independent organizational unit and are no longer part of the line organization. The advantage is that all relevant resources are available for achieving the project goals.
- Project society
  The purpose of the company is a project. In contrast to the pure project organization, which is only organizationally independent, the project society is additionally legally

Checklist resource plan / cost schedule

Project name		Project no.	
Responsible			
Version / Date		Status	

Question	Result
1. Is there as a basis for the resource plan / cost schedule a work breakdown structure (WBS)?	
2. For what period is the resource plan / cost schedule valid?	
3. Is it defined, when a target-actual comparison will be executed, and when updates are planned?	
4. Effort in the work packages	
a. Is the required communication for meetings and workshops considered?	
b. Are qualification needs and training requirements planned?	
c. Has it been considered that a project member optionally has to train new staff?	
d. Are quality measures like training, preparation, or revision of the results of one's own work, review activities, or lessons learned considered?	
5. Effort estimation	
a. Have the efforts been estimated by the project members themselves?	
b. Are there expert estimations, e.g., from systematic estimation workshops?	
c. Is there experience from similar projects that can be used?	
d. Have effort estimation procedures been used like COCOMO?	
6. Personnel planning	
a. Is there a recruitment plan (for external or internal staff)?	
b. Did the responsible manager agree to release resources for the project?	
c. Is there a plan for when which project members will be engaged in the project for what period of time?	
d. Is the capacity utilization balanced?	
e. Is it ensured that the workload per person is about 80 % in the long term, and if so, then does it only temporarily exceed 100 %?	
f. Are there reserves for a shortfall of personnel due?	
g. Has the workload resulting from other projects or line work been considered?	
7. Is there a spatial planning? Are there enough workspaces, meeting rooms, computers, office material? Has lead time been considered?	
8. Are there commitments for all required resources?	
9. Are there reserves for risks?	
10. Is the cost schedule consistent in the project (Sum of costs of the work packages to overall project costs, comparison of cost categories, accounts)?	

Fig. 3.22 Checklist for resource and cost planning

independent. It thus represents its own company, which was only created for one project. Well-known project companies are working groups, consortia, general contractors in the construction industry, in aerospace and research and development.

The choice of project organizational form depends on the size and type of the project, the corporate culture, the available resources and the urgency. In the respective companies, it is significant how strongly the project is integrated into the line organization. The less significant, the more independently a project can act.

The project organization includes all organizational units and regulations for the implementation of a project. It describes which roles there are in the project and how the roles relate to each other in the project. Each role is assigned tasks, competencies and responsibility and, finally, concrete project employees.

Project Roles and Committees
The typically important roles and committees in the project are:

- Principal
  The principal is the highest decision-making body in the project and makes the resources required by the project manager available. The principal has the most important role.
- Project manager, synonym: Project lead
  The project manager is responsible for achieving the project goals agreed with the principal.
- Project team
  The members of the project team are responsible to the project manager for the completion of the project's content work.
- Steering committee, synonyms: *Decision group, steering group, project committee* or *Review Board*
  If several organizations are affected by a project, they each send representatives to a steering ommittee. For organizational reasons, it is recommended that the project manager reports to the steering committee and that only the steering committee is authorized to give instructions to the project manager.

In larger projects, there is an additional role of the *Project Management Office (PMO)*. This role supports the project manager in the project, but also project members, mainly administratively, by agreement. Figure 3.23 shows how an overview of tasks and responsibilities of roles in the project can be displayed using a RACI matrix.

The project organization shows who reports to whom and who accepts which result. The following principle should apply in the project organization (see also Fig. 3.24):

ID	Tasks	Roles	Principal	Project manager	Project member 1	Project member 2	Project member 3	External consultant
1	Formulating project order		C	R				
2	Signing project order		A	A	I	I	I	
3	Situation analysis		I	A	R			
4	Project organization and optimization		I	A	I	I	I	C
5	Work package 1			A			R	C
6	Work package 2			A		C		R

R = Responsible - working on the task
A = Accountable - delegating and approving the work
C = Consulted - typically expert on subject
I = Informed - interested in progress

Fig. 3.23 Example for a RACI matrix

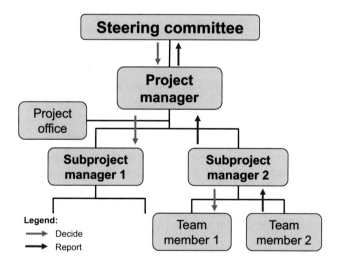

Fig. 3.24 Organizational chart with decision and reporting paths

- Top Down Decisions[1]
  Steering committee $\Rightarrow$ Project manager $\Rightarrow$ Subproject manager $\Rightarrow$ Project member
- Bottom Up Reports
  Steering committee $\Leftarrow$ Project manager $\Leftarrow$ Subproject manager $\Leftarrow$ Project member
  The following notes on the structure and layout of the project:

---

[1] See also Sect. 2.3.4.

- Manageable subprojects
  Depending on the size and complexity of the project, it is recommended to form several subprojects with corresponding subproject managers for the technical control, if necessary in several levels. Structure your project so that each subteam has a maximum of seven people.
- Social Mix
  The project experiences of the authors demonstrate that the more heterogeneous a team is, the more efficient it is. Therefore, we recommend that you bring together the following combinations:
  – Female and male
  – Old and young (experienced and new ideas)
  – Different nationalities
- Bringing together different competencies
  Try to bring broad knowledge into the teams:
  – Technical knowledge/commercial knowledge
  – Methodological knowledge/subject-specific knowledge
  – Generalists/experts
  – Practitioners/theorists
- Resource allocation for project employees
  In mixed organizations in particular, there can be a conflict of resources if project employees are "servants of two masters" because they have to fulfill a line function in addition to their project work. In this case, binding agreements are recommended, for example, how much of the weekly working time should be spent on project work. One possibility is the agreement of fixed days of the week for work in the project.
- Establishing of pairs
  The better the people in a project work together, the more successful the project. The intensive cooperation of two project employees in tandem can increase work efficiency. For example, a project member could carry out a task while another one reviews it at the same time with a subsequent change of roles. The pairs should be formed regularly and new ones should be formed again and again, so that a good cooperation in the project team results. For clarification, see also Fig. 2.7 on page 31.
- Establish connections in the line
  In matrix project organizations in particular, the project employees come from the line. Here it is worth involving many areas of the company in order to have the greatest possible access to company know-how.

Figure 3.24 shows a project organization chart with project roles, relationships between project roles, and communication paths in the project. In addition, it can list the different meetings and their frequency. Figure 3.25 shows a checklist for the project organization.

Checklist project organization

Project name		Project no.	
Responsible			
Version / Date		Status	

Question	Result
1. Does every project member know the principal?	
2. Is it clear who the project manager is?	
3. Project team	
a. Does everybody know who the members of the project team are?	
b. Are the tasks and roles of all team members defined in common and accepted by all?	
c. Are strengths and weaknesses in the team compensated?	
4. Project member	
a. Especially in a matrix project organization: Are project objectives and the involvement of employees in the project agreed on the corresponding responsible managers?	
b. Are all project members motivated? Do individuals' targets correspond to the targets of the project?	
c. Are all capabilities of the project members known?	
d. Do the capabilities of the project members match with the needs of the project?	
e. If capabilities are missing in the project: is it clear, how the required knowledge is to be developed or how external support can meet the needs?	
f. Are the tasks in the project clear?	
g. Is every project member able to spend the time needed for his tasks?	
h. Has every project member the competences required to complete his tasks? Have training measures been taken, when necessary?	

Fig. 3.25 Checklist project organization

3.2.7   Plan Optimization

During the planning process, there is always new information that needs to be considered. There can also be interactions: resources that are only available at certain times lead to other scheduling. It is recommended to use an iterative approach and repeatedly perform optimization steps to get closer to the "ideal plan".

There are the following optimization options:

- Resources
  - Vacation/absence planning
    The availability for the project should be optimized. Considerations include line tasks, tasks in other projects or absenteeism, such as vacation or training.
  - Compensation for overloading
    Overloading of project members is to be avoided.
- Terms
  - Benefits of network planning
    Network planning can be used to achieve a schedule optimization—the critical path determined with it shows the shortest possible duration.
  - Buffer planning
    Temporal buffers and risk premiums are to be considered for the schedule.
- Costs
  Even if the cost estimates can no longer be reduced, there is still a sensible procedure to follow in the project:
  - Start cost-intensive work packages later
  - Start risk-prone work packages earlier

If you follow this procedure, you can check the original cost estimates during the project. If there are deviations, the remaining cost estimates can be corrected based on the project costs incurred so far. In addition, an attempt is made to minimize the project costs incurred if it is apparent that the project is failing.

After the completion of the planning, the plans must be checked again during the implementation phase and corrected if necessary in order to prevent trying to fulfill outdated plans in the project.

3.2.8   Plan Alignment

Once the entire project plan has reached the appropriate level of maturity, it is time to coordinate with important stakeholders. For example, in a matrix project organization, communication with the superiors of the project employees about their work in the project is particularly important.

Finally, the plan must be coordinated with the principal. Depending on the project organization, the steering committee must also be involved. It is recommended to present interim versions of the plan beforehand in order to be able to react to suggestions for improvement, additional risks or criticism and to change the plan or find a compromise.

3.2.9 Project Kickoff

After the project planning work has been completed, the project kickoff is a key component of successful projects. The goals of the kickoff are:

- Conveying the project goal
- Information about the project plan
- Motivation
  - The project is important and the decision-makers support the project.
  - The project employees get to know each other.
  - Community feeling: This is how it can work!
- Start is clear: Conflicts are resolved, critical points are clarified.

In any case, take enough time for a successful project kickoff. It should be planned particularly well. If you save here, this usually takes its toll later in the project.

The entire project team should be present at the project kickoff. The supervisors of the project employees should also participate—they have to release their employees for the project and therefore be very well informed about the project. The more political the project, the more important this aspect is. You should be consistent here: If too many supervisors are missing for the kickoff, cancel the meeting! Give feedback to the principal and clarify the next steps.

For large projects, the project kickoff can be divided. First, a project opening meeting takes place and then the actual project kickoff with the principal. It is also possible to restrict the project kickoff to the core team with a smaller number of people. If necessary, a distinction must be made between an internal kickoff and an external kickoff if, for example, several companies are working together.

The first meeting already offers you an opportunity to lay the foundation for successful team work. The project members can get to know each other, create trust, align goals and expectations, and agree on a common approach in the project.

If you succeed in involving the individual team members personally, you can awaken the creative and constructive potential of the project team. Even good planning of the event location, for example externally, can prevent disruptions and distractions of the participants. The project kickoff gives you the opportunity to inspire all participants for the project at an early stage, create the conditions for a good project course and achieve constructive cooperation.

Topics of the kickoff meeting can be:

- Introductory round
- Official project opening with the principal
  Present the background and status of the project, presentation of future cooperation with the principal.
- Project goals: Why is there the project and the project team?
- Present the results of the planning:
  – Work breakdown structure
  – Time schedule with milestones
  – Cost plan
  – Presentation of risks
- Present the project organization, the project members with their tasks and responsibilities
- Explain the rules of the game in the project
- Communication
  Represent how communication takes place in the project, e.g. regular project and decision-maker meetings, status reports, reviews.
- Documentation
  – Agreements on documentation in the project such as calendars, reporting and protocols.
  – Define document management: Describe where project data is stored, for example: document management system, shared drive.
- Quality
  Describe the project quality objectives and how they are to be achieved.
- Tools
  Introduction of the tools used.
- Change management
  Presentation of the change management process.
- Outlook
  – Introducing the next milestone in detail.
  – Introducing the milestone after next in general terms.

Depending on the size of the project, a kickoff can take several hours or days. A multi-day kickoff can make sense if, for example, initial work is done, such as coordinating the next steps in the work package. The more extensive the project, the more external moderation is recommended.

3.2.10 Checklist

Figure 3.26 shows a checklist for the planning phase.

Checklist planning phase

Project name		Project no.	
Responsible			
Version / Date		Status	

Question	Result
1. Project objective	
a. Are the project goals and the subproject goals clear to everyone?	
b. Are all persons with necessary expertise involved?	
c. Can everybody optimally use his capabilities to achieve the project goals?	
2. Project plan	
a. Are all required plans available (work breakdown structure, time schedule, resource plan, cost schedule)?	
b. Is in each case the (temporal) matching of the plans ensured?	
c. Is the documentation of the project plan sufficiently voluminous?	
d. Is the project plan comprehensibly displayed in form of a presentation, a list, a bar chart, or similar?	
e. Has the project plan been jointly agreed by the project team?	
f. Has the project plan been communicated and is it accessible for the project staff?	
g. Does everybody know what has to be done with which expected result by when?	
h. Is it ensured that the project plan gets updated regularly? When will be the next version available?	
i. Is the duration and are the costs of the planning phase documented?	
3. Is the project organization clear?	
4. Are aspects of the project culture considered?	
5. Project communication	
a. Is the project communication controlled? Is there a communication plan?	
b. Is the communication in the project ensured so that every project member receives the information that they require?	
6. Project marketing	
a. Is the responsibility for project marketing assigned?	
b. Are project marketing activities defined?	
7. Are company-wide specifications, such as corporate identity and the usage of company-specific templates, fulfilled?	

Fig. 3.26 Checklist planning phase

3.3   Realization Phase

"The key to happiness lies in action, not in words."
Louis R. Hughes (*1949) Synonyms for the realization phaseare implementation phase
or *Execution phase*. This section describes how to control a project using milestones, meaningful controlling, and appropriate status and interim reports. Here, the traffic light logic has
proven to be a simple but effective tool. After working through this section, you will have
learned how to successfully carry out and control a well-planned project.

3.3.1   Goal and Results

The aim of the realization phase is to achieve the defined project goals. These project
goals are also dependent on the achieved result: This can be a service, a product, a document or something similar. Scope Management ensures that all project activities focus on
the implementation of the tasks from the work breakdown structure.

The goal is achieved with the successful acceptance of the project by the principal.
For technical projects, this may be the transfer of the developed product to the system
operation. Abstractly summarized, the result is:

- Project success
- Partial project success
- Project termination

3.3.2   Summary of Tasks

In order to successfully carry out the project, the following tasks must be fulfilled:

- Complete work packages
  The tasks should be completed within the agreed time frame with the resources made
  available.
- Control in case of deviations
  New tasks can arise or existing tasks can change due to deviations in the project.
  These must be distributed accordingly in the project. This can be done by the project
  manager himself or he delegates this accordingly, for example to the subproject man-
  agers.
- Carry out project controlling
  This ensures the achievement of the project's economic objectives.
- Update planning (dates, work packages)
  Dates and work packages are to be updated continuously.

Milestone management is demanding (see Sect. 3.3.3). A central aspect of project management is continuous communication (see Sect. 2.4), especially with the background knowledge that projects can fail due to poor communication. Regular communication should at least include:

- Regular meetings with the principal
- Regular project meetings
- Meetings between work groups
- Regular meetings with project members, if necessary in individual meetings

3.3.3 Milestones

Figure 3.27 shows that the structure of the realization phase for each milestone cycle is essentially a small project again. This means that the procedure from milestone to milestone corresponds to the procedure in a project with the phases strategy, planning, realization and closure.

During milestone cycles, one focuses on the goals associated with the respective milestone. The phase contents presented in this book are to be checked and usually only used to a limited extent as required. For example, in the strategy phase for a milestone, it should be clarified whether the current project order is still valid if, for example, the framework conditions have changed. For the planning of a milestone, no separate work breakdown structure and no additional project organization will be necessary. However, new work packages, changed work package contents or deadline shifts for work packages may result.

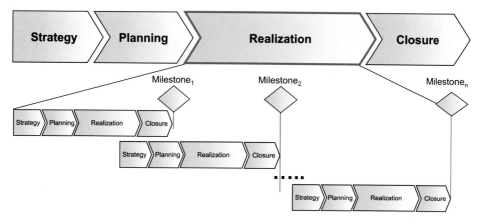

Fig. 3.27 Realization phase with milestones

The possible overlap must be taken into account—strategic/planning activities for the next milestone can already be carried out in parallel to realization work for the next milestone.

Milestone management includes:

- Preparing the milestone sessions
- Ensuring that the planned work results or the corresponding status are available for each milestone date
- Carrying out the milestone sessions
- Organizing the follow-up work from the milestone sessions
  - Protocol
  - Implementing one's own tasks
  - Monitoring other assigned tasks

Milestone sessions usually take place on the milestone date itself, in exceptional cases shortly before or shortly afterwards, and deal with the following content:

- Comprehensive information and presentation of the current state of the project to the participants, in particular to the steering committee.
- Acceptance of partial results, milestone results after presentation and review. It is also possible that there are updates or improvements to a work result. If these are larger volumes, the work result is to be presented again in a subsequent meeting.

In agile projects, it has been proven to be beneficial to plan or adjust the detailed planning of the next milestone after the completion of a milestone. The next milestone is to be planned in terms of time and at the level of headings. After the completion of a milestone, conflicts in terms of time and scope of the milestones are to be identified and clarified. Then the overall plan is to be adjusted.

3.3.4 Project Controlling

> "Everything that can be measured should be measured—and what cannot be measured should be made measurable."
>   *Galileo Galilei (1564–1642)*

Project Controlling
Project controlling according to DIN 69901-5 means the "ensuring of the achievement of all project goals by actual data capture, target-actual comparison, analysis of deviations, evaluation of deviations if necessary with correction suggestions, measure planning, control of the implementation of measures" [4].

Project controlling consists of the following three aspects:

- Project monitoring (*past of the project*)
  First of all, it must be determined what the status of the project is. Is the project still on schedule? What has been achieved so far? Any current difficulties must be made visible and analyzed. What are the causes of the difficulties, such as delays or increased resource consumption? Are there any indications of systematic problems that need to be resolved? What are the consequences of these difficulties?
- Project control activities (*present of the project*)
  If necessary, intervention must be made in the current project situation. Problems occurring problems are to be analyzed and solved, decisions are to be made.
- Trend analysis (*future of the project*)
  What is the further course of the project? If necessary, measures are to be taken such as the change of goals or the adaptation of the time schedule.

The goals of project controlling are:

- Always know the current degree of completion and the remaining expenses.
- Work well and make sure that all project members can work well.
- Always have an up-to-date plan.

Often the project management is supported by a project controller, for example, an external professional. He accompanies the project from the beginning. His main tasks are the analysis and reporting of the project situation as well as the evaluation of the project and the initiation of countermeasures if necessary. For this he needs social competence and experience in order to act appropriately in the team as well as methodical competence for a structured approach. Depending on the size of the project, project controlling can also be interpreted as a role and assigned to a project member.

3.3.5   Project Monitoring

Project monitoring is the prerequisite for efficient project control. The idea of project monitoring can be summarized in the following questions: What do we want? Where are we?

It is recommended to compare the planned and actual results on a regular basis. This can be done, for example, once a month or at milestones. A short daily exchange in the project team is also conceivable, similar to the Daily Scrum (described in Sect. 4.2.4 with further details in Sect. 4.3). Project monitoring includes:

- Target-actual comparison
  There are, for example, the following possibilities:
  - Use of project key figures

- Progress in content—Progress control oriented towards project goals
- Schedule control—based on the time schedule
- Cost control—based on the cost schedule
- Presentation of the progress of the project
  Status or interim reports are recommended.
- Milestone management
  Within the framework of milestones or quality gate reviews, the current project status is intensively reflected. The project employees are informed and asked to prepare the work results accordingly in good time before the milestone. The milestone session is prepared, carried out and documented. Subsequently, due follow-up work and identified tasks are to be carried out and their implementation is to be monitored.
- Considering change requests
  Section 2.2.3 describes the handling of changes in the project. It is recommended to collect and prepare the most important ones for a milestone date if they can have a major impact on the further course of the project. These can then be discussed specifically and it can be decided how to proceed.

Content-Related Progress

The biggest challenge in project controlling in terms of comparing planned with actual results is the control of the progress of work in order to be able to measure the progress of the project. It is both the most important and the most difficult monitoring task. How can the degree of completion of a work package be determined? Measuring the degree of completion in percentages is tricky and dangerous. The "90% trap" is well known: At a certain point in time, a project employee believes that 90% of the project result has already been achieved. This is explained by the fact that the solution path is known, but the "unforeseen" is not. As a result, despite the clear solution path, there are often still high costs, because disruptions and problems not taken into account delay implementation. Therefore, the estimation of effort is particularly critical to question and possibly increase significantly, especially for inexperienced project employees.

Without professional expertise, it is hardly possible to measure the progress of work, as the respective projects are too different. Since this book deals with the general topic of project management, it is not possible to go into the different professional matters and possible measures of different projects here.

A project manager must bring the respective project-specific professional skills. Specialist knowledge is necessary so that progress control can be based on professional facts. Procedure:

- Define measures and criteria together with the responsible person.
- Evaluate the quality of the current state using maturity levels (status information).
- In the simplest case, only the statuses "In Progress" and "Completed" are used.

Presentation of the Project Progress

Progress on the project is usually represented with status reports, preferably on a regular basis every two to four weeks, depending on the priority/criticality, size and duration of the project. The status reports should relate to the project objectives and present the current level of achievement. On the one hand, they serve to inform the principal, on the other hand they protect the project team: What have we achieved so far? Are we still on the right track? In addition to the target-actual comparison, for example in the form of project key figures, a simple color display is often used with the traffic light logic (Fig. 3.28):

- Traffic light color **Red**: escalation required
  There are serious difficulties, an escalation to the next level of responsibility is required.
- Traffic light color **Yellow**: Critical
  There are problems that can be solved within the affected organizational unit.
- Traffic light color **Green**: Okay
  Everything is on track, any problems that have arisen can be resolved within the normal workflows.

This traffic light logic can be used at all levels of the project: For the project itself, the subprojects and the work packages.

3.3.6   Project Control Activities

In addition to project planning, project control activities are the central task of project management. Good project control ensures that the project is carried out as planned. The project should be carried out as effectively and efficiently as possible. Effective means:

Fig. 3.28   Traffic light logic

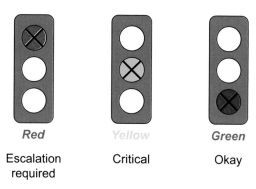

Red	Yellow	Green
Escalation required	Critical	Okay

The goal is achieved. Efficient means: The goal is achieved with the optimal use of time and resources. Project management includes:

- Determining the project completion or requesting the project cancellation
  The main goal is of course a successful project completion. But even if a project has to be canceled, it is the noble task of a project manager to admit this honestly and to request a project cancellation accordingly (see Sect. 2.3.8).
- Acceptance of (partial) results of work packages
  Work packages as central units in the project are to be overviewed and supervised by the project manager. The goal is the acceptance of the results of the work packages. In addition, the project manager starts, accompanies (for example, in case of changes) and ends the work packages.
- Representation of results and status, presentations
  This is part of project communication and helps to present the project well and show the participants the successes. This can positively influence the project culture. The minimum scope is the activities and results achieved during the reporting period and the next planned activities.
  If there are changes to the plan, these must be shown and justified rationally. It makes sense that changes to the plan are worked out in advance and the consequences for the project are transparent. If necessary, follow-up activities will arise with regard to planning and optimization.
- Conflict management in case of disruptions
  It is important to address conflicts as early as possible, to deal with the parties to the conflict and to work out a solution. There should be clear separation between the personal and the professional. It is helpful to clearly identify the similarities and the conflicts. The differences should be shown with the respective advantages and disadvantages. The project manager should then make a decision if necessary. Defined escalation paths are to be observed. Depending on the project organization, the line manager can be involved in the conflict resolution. If necessary, external help can be requested.
- Change management
  Change requests during the implementation can have a significant impact on a project (see Sect. 2.2).
- Risk management
  The project manager should regularly review the risks, assess them and take appropriate measures. It is important to identify unknown risks in good time (see also Sect. 2.7).
- Leading the project employees
  Leading project employees differs from leading employees in the line organization. A project manager gives professional guidelines, but usually has no authority to give orders. Depending on the project organization and corporate culture, the project manager is often authorized to establish professional guidelines and tell the employees

which tasks they will work on in the project. A leadership with goals that come from work packages has proven itself (see also Sect. 2.3).

- Task force

  Forming a task force can be a useful way to solve complex problems. The causes can be manifold: the work to be done in a work package was massively underestimated, unforeseeable technical problems arise or an important project collaborator falls ill. The idea is to form a "team within a team" over a defined period of time and bring it together in a project room. The task force should define a specific goal for the given problem. There is a daily communication with management to support the task force effectively. After reaching the goal, the task force can be dissolved again.

  Often, the necessary use of a task force points to structural problems in the project. Therefore, the task force should be an exception in the project. There is a danger that, by focusing on a problem, other project topics will be neglected. In the worst case, one fire is extinguished, but new fires arise in other places.

  Example: In an IT project, processes tests are to be carried out using a system. A prerequisite for this are functioning interfaces between three system components. One project employee is responsible for these interfaces with 50% of her working time. The project manager receives the information that the interfaces do not work yet. In a conversation between the project manager and the project employee, the following tasks were identified, which were not considered in the project plan:

  1. The interfaces must be delivered and set up.
  2. The currently valid interface specification is to be checked.
  3. It is to be checked whether the interfaces have been developed according to the currently valid interface specification.
  4. Test data is to be created according to the interface specifications.
  5. Dates must be coordinated with the responsible persons for the three system components for installation and testing.
  6. Access to the test environment must be coordinated with other stakeholders.
  7. If errors are found, they must be analyzed and corrected.

  Since the topic of interfaces has turned out to be a bottleneck in the project, the project manager decides to set up a *task force*. Two project employees and the responsible persons for the three system components support the interface responsible person for 14 days in order to get the interfaces up and running. A daily regular communication is set up for coordination of the work.

- Request/accompany project review

  A regular project review can help prevent a crisis situation in good time, but also ensure that the project is on the right track. It can be carried out, for example, by internal audit, but often a look from the outside with the help of an external auditor (see also page 46) is also helpful. For long-term projects, a regular review is recommended at least once a year.

3.3.7   Trend Analysis

The task of the project manager is not only to determine and analyze the current situation in the project and to control the project, but also to look into the future. For example, it is important to find out whether the project can still be carried out as planned or whether the planning has to be adapted. The trend analysis with the following content helps here:

- Prediction of project course
  This takes into account findings in the project and includes the communication of these as well as the search for possible solutions with the corresponding decision.
- Ongoing update and correction of the project plan
  This is a continuous process in reaction to project-disrupting events and new findings.

The milestone trend analysis (MTA) is a special form of trend analysis, which is based on the milestone plan. The goal is to monitor the progress of the project and to detect delays in schedules at an early stage. Based on the milestone plan, the agreed deadlines and the current status of the work results are checked regularly.

An example is shown in Fig. 3.29 with report deadlines on the x-axis and corresponding milestone deadlines on the y-axis. In January 2022 (x-axis) there are the following planned dates:

- Milestone 1 **Strategy**: May 2022
- Milestone 2 **Specification**: September 2022
- Milestone 3 **Closure** : November 2022

The course of the milestones can be interpreted as follows:

- Milestone 1 **Strategy** (lower yellow line, starting May 2022):
  The course of the milestone term-series is ideal. The time estimates were continuously confirmed and the planned time was met.
- Milestone 2 **Specification** (middle green line, starting September 2022):
  The course of the milestone term-series falls. It is possible that too much buffer was planned, the milestone will be reached earlier than planned.
- Milestone 3 **Completion** (upper red line, starting November 2022):
  This milestone course shows too optimistic a time planning. The originally planned time could not be kept and had to be postponed several times.

In regular meetings with responsible persons and participants, the status is reported according to the milestones, preferably within the milestone meetings themselves.

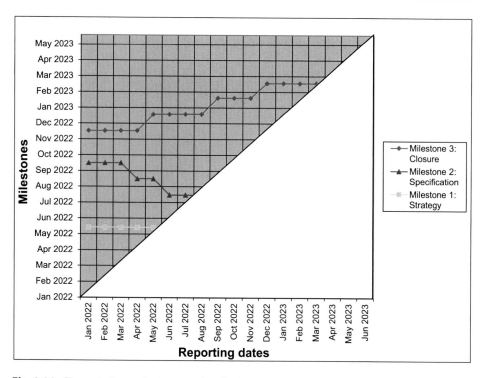

Fig. 3.29   Example for a milestone trend analysis

3.3.8   Checklist

Figure 3.30 shows a checklist for the realization phase.

3.4   Closure Phase

"The outcome gives the actions their titles."

Johann Wolfgang von Goethe (1749–1832) This section describes the final activities in the project: the project closure. The most important thing is the handover of the project result with the acceptance by the principal, which can also be done partially. Completion activities are concerned with the result assurance and the (stepwise) dissolution of the project team.

3.4.1   Goal and Results

Project Closure
The project closure is the formal end of a project. All activities in the project context are terminated. According to DIN 69901-5, the "closure phase" includes the "set of activities and processes for the formal termination of a project" [4].

Checklist realization phase

Project name		Project no.	
Responsible			
Version / Date		Status	

Question	Result
1. Regular consideration of the project with regard to objectives or attainment	
a. Is it checked what (sub-) goals have been reached already?	
b. Are measures defined if (sub-) goals have not been reached yet?	
c. Do all project activities serve the attainment?	
2. Next project activities Are the tasks to be done by the next milestone clear? Are the objectives clear for the next but one milestone?	
3. Project status – Is the project still in budget, in time, and in quality?	
a. What is the current project status, especially related to the milestones?	
b. Is there a target-actual comparison concerning structure, duration, and costs of the project?	
c. Is there a project documentation containing project progress reports, minutes, decisions, and agreements?	
4. Working in the project	
a. Is every team member able to finish their tasks successfully?	
b. Are pending problems being examined or escalated if required?	
c. How are working results examined and saved?	
d. Are there project specific training activities?	
5. Project communication	
a. Are all stakeholders adequately involved or informed?	
b. Are there regular recorded project status meetings?	
6. Project team / project culture	
a. Are there activities for people entering and leaving the project?	
b. Are there team building activities to improve the project culture?	
7. Regular risk management	
a. Are new risks identified? Are new and known risks processed?	
b. Are existing risks in discussion with the principal and the project team? Are measures defined and examined?	
c. Are risk probabilities of incidence and estimated impacts updated?	
8. Continuous project marketing	
a. Are project marketing activities executed?	
b. Will information get outside the project, for instance, to other departments or customers?	

Fig. 3.30 Checklist realization phase

At the end of the closure phase of a successful project, the release of the project team with the acceptance of the project result. The activities and results of the project are documented in a final report. Finally, the project team is dissolved and the resources are released.

3.4.2   Acceptance

The acceptance process can be divided into four phases:

1. Presentation of the project result
   The principal will be presented with the project result. Depending on the type of project, she or he will receive:
   - Product
   - Product documentation
   - Final report
     This contains the most important information about the project:
     - Project assignment
     - Management Summary
       What was achieved? How was the project planned and carried out?
     - Project result
       To what extent was the goal achieved?
       Which solution paths were pursued?
       What effort (time, cost or resources) was required?
     You will find a template for a project final report in Sect. 6.17 on page 181.
2. Approval
   The principal signs the final report and thus formally releases the project with confirmation:
   - Degree of achievement of the goal
   - Delivered quality
   - Amount of the costs
   - Required time
   If necessary, the principal grants partial release and remedial measures are agreed, each with responsibility and target date.
3. Transition of the project result
   The transfer regulation is dependent on the project and project result. This can even be separate (partial) projects, which have to be dealt with during the project realization. The following transfer scenarios are conceivable:
   - Handover to service/operation
     …with integration, adjustments, instruction of the hotline, training of employees, creation/transfer of an operating manual, etc.
   - Transfer to the line organization
     A separate department is responsible for the operation and further development.

- Migration
  Migration of data from the legacy system to the new system.
- Transfer to an introductory project
  Especially in a larger organization, it can be necessary with hundreds of affected persons to plan and carry out the introduction step by step over a longer period of time with:
  – Pilot phase
  – Gradual expansion of the user base
  – Rollout/live operation: complete launch

4. Final phase
   It should be clarified who the contact person for project topics will be after project completion. Example: Problems with errors in the software that are only discovered by the customer after release. Ideas for this are:
   - Step-by-step shutdown of the project with the retention of an ever-decreasing project team.
   - Definition of a follow-up project from suitable project members.

3.4.3 Final Documentation and Lessons Learned

A project is successfully completed with the acceptance by the principal. Nevertheless, there are still important things to do in order to learn for the future. Feedback helps to reflect the positive and negative aspects of the project. Results of the closure phase are:

- Lessons learned workshop/feedback
  In a reflection, the principal and the project team should work out what went well in the project and what should be done better in future projects. This can be done in one meeting or in separate meetings. Each project participant should give feedback on what they have learned and what positive and negative experiences have been made.
- Final report
  A final project report is helpful for further projects in the company, the lessons learned are the basis for a learning organization.
- Final presentation from the final report
  This presentation contains a summary of project contents as well as the most important findings from the lessons-learned workshop.
- Final Meeting
  Possible agenda:
  – Introduce the final presentation
  – Show the next steps
  – Hand over the final documentation to the principal
- Depositing the final documentation in a corporate knowledge base
  The aim is to systematically secure the experiences made in the project. Every (future) project manager should have access to this knowledge base. In doing so, the failed projects should also be taken into account, because there is much to learn from them.

In addition, it makes sense for project managers to exchange and present their projects to each other. In this way, the knowledge about project management, for example, can be increased within a company.

3.4.4   Dissolving

A project is characterized by a beginning and a clearly defined end. With the completion of the project, the project manager and the project team end their activities. The committees are dissolved. There is a release of project resources, for example for other new projects. As a rule, the resources are gradually reduced. Certain project members take care of possible follow-up projects. In IT projects, for example, part of the project team still accompanies the transition to operation. At the latest at this point, if not yet done, the result security should be carried out. A nice party offers a good emotional closure (Fig. 3.31). Final business activity is the closing of the project cost center.

3.4.5   Outlook

At the end of the project, it makes sense to look beyond the horizon. What could a meaningful follow-up project look like? What is possible to expand or further improve the project result? For IT projects: Who develops the software or the product further? Who incorporates changes, who eliminates errors? If, for example, a product is introduced to the market, possible follow-up projects include:

- Financial services for the purchase of the product (financing, leasing)
- Service for the product (maintenance, repair)

Often, a good cooperation develops between the project members in projects. It makes sense to keep an experienced team ("Never change a winning team"). In this way, you can try to assign the entire team to a new project in order to use synergy effects.

3.4.6   Checklist

Figure 3.32 shows a checklist for the closure phase.

Fig. 3.31 Project completion

Checklist closure phase

Project name		Project no.	
Responsible			
Version / Date		Status	

Question	Result
1. Project acceptance	
a. Has the principal approved the project? If there is a partial acceptance with required repairs: are measures defined with responsibilities and due dates?	
b. Are the project results delivered including project documentation?	
c. Has the principal formally discharged the project?	
2. Project documentation	
a. Is there an acceptance report?	
b. Is there a project closure report including all open points?	
c. Are the project duration and costs (final invoice) documented including a target-actual comparison?	
d. Has the project set-up been documented?	
3. Final meeting	
a. Is there a feedback from the principal and the project team?	
b. Has a project review with consideration of lessons learned been conducted?	
c. Has it been documented what went well in the project, what avoidable mistakes have been made, and what to improve in future?	
4. Was there an emotional completion with dissolution of the project like a closing ceremony?	
5. Project dissolution	
a. Have the project members been released, for instance, transferred to other projects or back into the line organization?	
b. Are employment contracts or contracts with partners terminated?	
c. Has the cost center been closed?	
d. Has the final completion been communicated?	
6. Post project phase	
a. Are there agreements for remaining tasks?	
b. Who is responsible for further support or implementation?	
c. Has the transition to the line organization, specialist department, or operation department been organized?	
d. Are there corresponding documents like an operational manual?	
e. Are there practical follow-up projects?	
7. Has the project know-how been transferred for future projects, e.g., by an entry into a project database?	

Fig. 3.32   Checklist closure phase

3.5 Summary

A project can be divided into project phases. There are different structuring options with different names in the literature, as well as company-specific names. For this book, the following four practice-oriented phases are defined:

- Strategy phase
  The strategy phase begins with an analysis of the situation and environment in order to determine the framework conditions for a project to be carried out. If a project becomes concrete, the objectives are defined. Initial solutions complete the basics for a project assignment. The project assignment stands for the start of a project. Depending on the size and type of the project, the creation of a requirements and duties specification is required.
- Planning phase
  Project planning is a key task of the project manager. The result of project planning is the project plan, which includes further plans. The most important plans are the work breakdown structure (WBS) and the schedule including milestone plan and resource and cost plan based on it. The task of project organization is to find an optimal structure in interaction with the line organization for a successful implementation of the project. Corresponding roles and committees are to be defined.
- Realization phase
  The controlling of a project is another key task of the project manager. The focus is on the organization of the acceptance of intermediate milestones, the project completion or—if necessary—the project termination. Other priorities are ensuring communication within the project and with the stakeholders, as well as activities in case of disruptions in the project course. Based on the milestone plan, the project progress can be controlled and possible schedule difficulties can be identified using milestone trend analysis.
- Closure phase
  In this phase, the project is completed, the central point is the acceptance of the project by the principle. In a post-phase, final work, handovers and the release of resources take place. Lessons learned and a final report secure the knowledge acquired for future projects.

3.6 Problems

3.1 Project Goals
(a) What do you understand by a goal definition?
(b) Target operationalization: What does a target description include?
(c) Why are project goals important?

(d) What should you definitely pay attention to when describing the goals?

(e) Which methods can you use to find project goals?

3.2 Environment Analysis

(a) What methods can you use for the environment analysis?

(b) What are possible problems in the environment analysis?

(c) What is the difference between the environment analysis and the risk analysis?

3.3 Milestones

(a) What is a milestone?

(b) Why are milestones necessary in a project?

3.4 Project Plan

What are the most important plans summarized in the project plan?

   Explain these briefly.

3.5 Work Breakdown Structure (WBS)

(a) Describe the content and purpose of the work breakdown structure.

(b) How can a work breakdown structure be created? When should which different pro-
     cedure be used?

(c) Explain how a work breakdown structure can be structured.

(d) What advantages does a WBS offer?

(e) What are the limits of the WBS?

3.6 Resource plan and cost schedule

What is the benefit of a resource plan and cost schedule?

3.7 Project organization

(a) List the organization forms you know.

(b) What questions should a project organization chart answer?

3.8 Project organization—Assessment

(a) Is a line organization suitable for carrying out a project?

(b) What are the advantages of a project organization?

3.9 Project controlling

(a) What do you understand by project controlling?

(b) What does project controlling require and what does it include?

3.10 Traffic Light Logic

Explain how traffic light logic can be used in status reports.

3.11 Closure Phase

Why is project acceptance closely linked to change management?

References

1. Angermeier, G.: Projektmagazin Projektmanagement-Glossar (2020). https://www.projekt-magazin.de/glossarterm. Accessed: 23 Aug 2022
2. Atlassian: Jira (2020). https://www.atlassian.com/software/jira. Accessed 23 Aug 2022
3. DIN Deutsches Institut für Normung e. V.: DIN 69900:2009-01, Projektmanagement – Netzplantechnik; Beschreibungen und Begriffe (2009). https://www.beuth.de/en/standard/din-69900/113428266. Accessed: 23 Aug 2022
4. DIN Deutsches Institut für Normung e. V.: DIN 69901-5:2009-01, Projektmanagement – Projektmanagementsysteme – Teil 5: Begriffe (2009). https://www.beuth.de/en/standard/din-69901-5/113428752. Accessed: 23 Aug 2022
5. Drucker, P.F.: People and Performance: The Best of Peter Drucker on Management. Harper's College Press, New York (1977)
6. Gabler Wirtschaftslexikon: Balanced Scorecard (2018). https://wirtschaftslexikon.gabler.de/definition/balanced-scorecard-28000/version-251640. Accessed: 23 Aug 2022
7. International Organization for Standardization (ISO): ISO/IEC 25000:2014 Systems and software engineering. Systems and software Quality Requirements and Evaluation (SQuaRE) – Guide to SQuaRE. Tech. rep., International Organization for Standardization (ISO) (2018). https://www.iso.org/standard/72089.html. Accessed: 23 Aug 2022
8. International Organization for Standardization (ISO): ISO/IEC/IEEE 29148:2018 Systems and software engineering – Life cycle processes – Requirements engineering. Tech. rep., International Organization for Standardization (ISO) (2018). https://www.iso.org/standard/72089.html. Accessed: 23 Aug 2022
9. Microsoft: MS Project (2020). https://www.microsoft.com/de-DE/microsoft-365/project/project-management-software. Accessed: 23 Aug 2022
10. Project Management Institute: A Guide to the Project Management Body of Knowledge (PMBOK Guide 6), 6th edn. Project Management Institute (2017)
11. projectlibre.com: ProjectLibre (2020). http://www.projectlibre.com/. Accessed: 23 Aug 2022
12. reimus.NET GmbH: Controlling-Portal.de – Die Nutzwertanalyse (2022). https://www.controllingportal.de/Fachinfo/Grundlagen/Die-Nutzwertanalyse.html. Accessed: 23 Aug 2022
13. Sackman, H.: Delphi Assessment: Expert Opinion, Forecasting, and Group Process (1974). https://www.rand.org/content/dam/rand/pubs/reports/2006/R1283.pdf. Accessed: 23 Aug 2022
14. Stickel, E., Groffmann, H.D., Rau, K.H.: Gabler Wirtschaftsinformatiklexikon. Springer Fachmedien Wiesbaden GmbH (1997)
15. Zangemeister, C.: Nutzwertanalyse in der Systemtechnik – Eine Methodik zur multidimensionalen Bewertung von Projektalternativen. Zangemeister & Partner (2014)

Agility in Projects

4

The introduction of agility initially resulted in a paradigm shift in the IT environment. The agile approach is based on agile software development. The Manifesto for Agile Software Development [2] emphasises the following values:

- Individuals and interactions more than processes and tools
- Working software more than comprehensive documentation
- Collaboration with the customer more than contract negotiation
- Responding to change more than following a plan

Agile Software Development
Agile software development includes various approaches to software development in which requirements and solutions arise through the collaboration of self-organized and cross-functional teams with their customers and end users [5].

In traditional projects, a product or service is completed at the end of the project after a significant period of time. In agile projects, however, a product or service is created in smaller parts in defined cycles. Agile processes are iterative and incremental. They can quickly adapt to changed conditions.

Agility
Agility is the ability of an organization's information function to make preparations to respond very quickly, preferably in real time, to changing capacity requirements as well as changed functional requirements, and to use the possibilities of

© Springer-Verlag GmbH Germany, part of Springer Nature 2022
D. Alam and U. Gühl, *Project Management for Practice*,
https://doi.org/10.1007/978-3-662-65159-9_4

information technology in such a way that the professional scope of the organization can be extended or even redesigned (according to Dominic Lindner [13]).

Let's look at the most important aspects in connection with agility (according to [13]):

- Speed
  In the project, one would like to be able to react quickly to changes. Tasks are planned and implemented in regular, short cycles.
- Adaptation
  Adaptations are made in response to changed requirements/conditions. With the help of continuous improvement, this not only affects the project results, but also the approach in the project.
- Flexibility
  Project participants are usually well trained and can be used flexibly for different project tasks. For example, project employees who describe requirements can work as testers in a later cycle.
- Dynamics
  In the agile environment, dynamics stand for the mobility of a project member, of his own accord, to change his position in the project.
- Networking
  It is important to have continuous communication between project participants. This should be supported by spatial and technical aspects.
  - Spatially
    There is a project house or a project room where all project participants come together, either permanently or temporarily. The project participants should meet regularly and be able to communicate directly.
  - Technical
    As support, virtual conference rooms, video or telephone conferences, chats and Internet-accessible access to project-relevant information and shared resources can be used.
- Trust
  A culture of trust with flat hierarchies increases the job satisfaction of project participants and leads to better project results.
- Self-organization
  Agile projects are characterized by short decision-making processes, support of creativity and autonomous work groups.

The motivation for agile project management is the expectation that this will enable more projects to be successfully implemented. According to the "Chaos Manifesto 2011", this has also been confirmed: for projects in which application software was developed using agile methods instead of the waterfall method, the success probability is three times as high (42% compared to 14%) []20, page 25]. Companies that switch to agile methods generally do not return to traditional methods. This is taken as an indication that the use of agile methods has a positive effect on corporate success [23]. Similarly, according to participants in the study, "Status Quo (Scaled) Agile (2019/20)" [11], the success rate of agile methods is significantly more positive than that of traditional project management. The most important reasons for the application of agile methods are:

- Shorter product introduction time,
- Optimization of quality,
- Reduction of project risks.

Agile methods are used primarily in software development. However, the participants in the above mentioned study also said that they use them in IT-related (52%) or non-IT related activities (39%). The reasons for the use of agile methods are illustrated by a survey by CollabNet VersionOne [4], conducted between August and December 2018 with 1,319 responses, shown in Table 4.1 (Multiple responses were possible).

According to the same survey, as shown in Fig. 4.1, the most used method is Scrum [4]. The use of Scrum in combination with XP (Extreme Programming) was mentioned by 10%. Often, a mixture of different agile methods is used (14%). Other agile methods mentioned include Kanban, Scrumban and Lean Startup.

The survey also looked at which agile techniques are used [4]. The most used were (percentages according to frequency of occurrence – multiple mentions were possible):

Table 4.1 Reasons for using agile methods

No.	Reason	Percent (%)
1.	Accelerated software delivery	74
2.	Improved change management	62
3.	Increased productivity	51
4.	Improved alignment between business and IT	50
5.	Increased software quality	43
6.	Increasing the predictability of deliveries	43
7.	Improving the project's external image	42
8.	Reducing project costs	41
9.	Improving team spirit	34
10.	Reducing project risks	28
11.	Improving engineering discipline	23
12.	Increasing the maintainability of software	21
13.	Better management of distributed teams	19

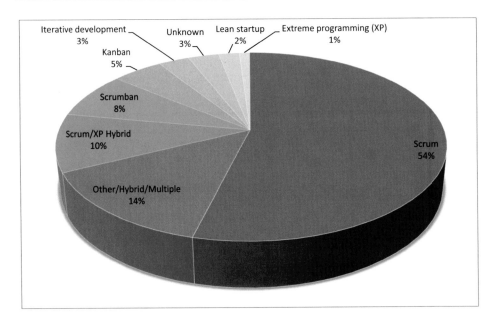

Fig. 4.1 Agile methods used

1. Daily Standup (86%)
2. Sprint/iteration planning (80%)
3. Retrospective (80%)
4. Sprint/iteration review (80%)
5. Short iterations (67%)

Table 4.2 shows the most frequently mentioned agile practices according to the study by Koblenz University of Applied Sciences (multiple answers were possible) [11, slide 84]. In addition, it contains references to sections in this book that explain the practices mentioned in more detail.

nDecisions about which agile methods and techniques are used depends on the project and corporate culture. Sect. 4.1 introduces the practices of Extreme Programming – the basis of many agile processes. Sect. 4.2 focuses on Scrum, the most used agile method. Other important agile methods are:

- Kanban
  Kanban is part of the Toyota Production System and is used to optimize production processes [15]. This leads to lower inventory costs and justified the "just in time" principle. The method was adapted for software development and later for general

Table 4.2 Most commonly used agile practices

No.	Agile Practices	Percent (%)	Refer to, see
1.	Sprint Planning	82	Sect. 4.2.3
2.	Daily Scrum	82	Sect. 4.2.4, page 140
3.	User Stories	80	Sect. 4.2.2, page 132
4.	Product Backlog	80	Sect. 4.2.2, page 134
5.	Sprint Backlog	78	Sect. 4.2.3, page 135
6.	Sprint Review	78	Sect. 4.2.5
7.	Sprint Retrospective	77	Sect. 4.2.6
8.	Kanban Board	77	see below

project management [12]. It is based on a Kanban board with columns and rows in which processes are modeled. The procedure includes the following steps:

1. First, the process is visualized with its activities. There is one column for each activity. The work to be done is divided into tasks. Each task is written on a card and placed under the corresponding column (compare with Task Board, page 140).
2. Then the *work in progress limit* is defined. This means that the number of tasks that can be assigned to one process activity is limited.
3. Finally, the *lead time* is measured, which is the time required for a task to go through the process.

Based on this information, processes are improved in order to optimize throughput time and make it predictable. Kanban can be used effectively for service organizations, such as first level support or a user help desk.

- Scrumban

  This is a hybrid form. Based on Scrum, there is a continuous process improvement with the methods from Kanban. This makes it possible to simplify the planning process, for example. In Scrum, the costs for prioritized entries from the product backlog, which are to be transferred to the sprint backlog, are estimated individually in each case (see Sect. 4.2.3). In Scrumban, a fixed number of entries from the product backlog are transferred to the sprint backlog instead. The prerequisite for this is that the entries each have a defined scope and are sufficiently well formulated. Ajay Reddy describes this approach in detail [16].

- Lean Startup

  Eric Ries developed the Lean Startup method [17]. It originally aimed at developing companies and products with the goal of getting feedback as early as possible to see if a business model is feasible. Its principle is an iterative build-measure-learn loop. First, a product with basic functionality is developed as quickly as possible. This is known as *Minimal Viable Product (MVP)*. Then, based on customer feedback, further development or change takes place. After the next completion, the product is checked again and the next iteration begins.

4.1   Extreme Programming (XP)

"Do the simplest thing that could possibly work."

*Kent Beck (*1961)* Extreme Programming (XP) is a software development methodology with the goal of improving the quality of software and the responsiveness to changing customer requirements. XP was originally defined with twelve practices (Fig. 4.2), which are briefly explained below [1].

1. Planning game

   Planning takes place at the beginning of each development phase. The client and the team discuss the work done so far, the client gives feedback. According to priorities, the client then presents desired requirements, usually with index cards. The team estimates the effort required in each case and determines how much can be realised by the end of the iteration.

2. Small releases

   Functioning programs and updates are to be presented to the customer as early as possible so that he can give feedback and make criticisms and suggestions quickly. Errors, unwanted behavior or change requests can be detected and considered for the next delivery more quickly in this way. Fixed release cycles with a duration of about four weeks are proposed.

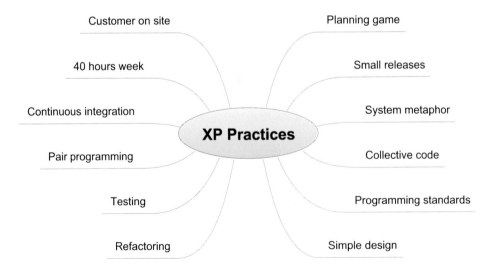

Fig. 4.2 XP-practices

3. System metaphor

   Instead of a complex system architecture, a simple metaphor is used, which illustrates the functioning of the system to every project participant. This makes it easier to understand the basic components and their relationships.

4. Collective code

   Everyone is allowed to change the code anywhere. The whole team is responsible for the code.

5. Programming standards

   Everyone uses the same standard so that the team can work well together and also find their way around in the code of others.

6. Simple design

   Only what is actually needed for the implementation of the requirements should be implemented. Unnecessary complexity as well as duplications are to be avoided. Code that is no longer used should be deleted.

7. Refactoring

   Whenever it is clear that the software design can be improved, it should be done. The goal is a better understanding of the code, easier maintainability and reduced susceptibility to errors. Automated component tests ensure that implemented functionality still works and has no side effects.

8. Testing

   In test-driven development, developers write component tests before they implement code. These are automated and serve as regression tests in continuous integration and refactoring to ensure that there are no side effects. The customer defines functional tests in parallel.

9. P *air programming*

   Following the four-eyes principle, two developers work on the code at the same time. One developer writes the code, the other checks it in parallel, asks questions, makes suggestions for improvement and points out errors. After a while, the roles are reversed. This approach has the disadvantage of higher expenditure, but it results in higher code quality.

10. Continuous integration

    All changes of each developer should be integrated into the overall project continuously, or at least daily. Automated component tests must continue to run after each integration. In this way, the individual changes or extensions are checked throughout and all developers work with the latest version.

11. 40 hours week

    The well-being of the developers is important. No overtime should be worked.

12. Customer on site

    The customer or a representative should be a permanent part of the team. This makes it possible to give feedback on a regular basis, to answer questions quickly or to bring in ideas and priorities.

These practices have since evolved, but can also be found in other agile approaches.

4.2   Scrum

"A hiker is not someone who sometimes walks slowly and sometimes quickly.
   A hiker is someone who walks steadily and purposefully."
   Chawadsche Abdullah Ansari, also known as Pir-e Herat (1006–1089) Scrum, developed by Ken Schwaber and Jeff Sutherland, is an iterative, incremental framework for project management [18] and currently the standard approach in agile software development. According to the study "Status Quo (Scaled) Agile 2020", Scrum is the most important agile approach and is rated as important or very important by more than 80% of respondents [11, slide 52]. The Scrum Guide, available in various languages, is the official reference for Scrum [19]. The basis of the approach with Scrum is the understanding that, on the one hand, a customer changes his or her opinion about what he or she wants or needs, and on the other hand, unforeseen problems arise that cannot be taken into account in the planning. Scrum provides for self-organized and interdisciplinary teams to work closely together with regular communication in defined time boxes to deliver working products.

This section describes the use of Scrum in the practice of the authors. The following roles (Sect. 4.2.1) and three artifacts are introduced:

- Product Backlog (Sect.4.2.2)
- Sprint Backlog (Sect. 4.2.3)
- Increment (Sect. 4.2.4)
Scrum events are another important part of Scrum. The central event is the sprint. This includes the events:

- Sprint Planning (Sect. 4.2.3),
- Daily Scrum (Sect. 4.2.4),
- Sprint Review (Sect. 4.2.5),
- Sprint Retrospective (Sect. 4.2.6).
An overview is shown in Fig. 4.3.

4.2.1   Roles

The Scrum team distinguishes the following roles (Fig. 4.4):

- Product Owner
  The product owner is responsible for formulating requirements in the form of user stories in the customer role. User stories are listed in the product backlog according to priority. In addition, the product owner is available for questions and decisions regarding the user stories.

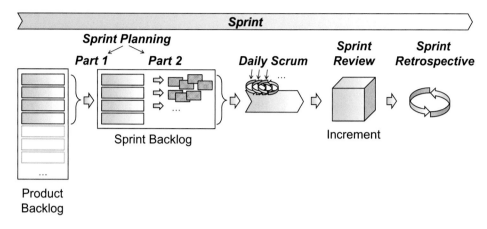

Fig. 4.3   Scrum with events and artifacts

Fig. 4.4   Scrum team

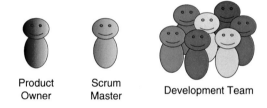

- Scrum master
  The Scrum master is responsible for ensuring that the Scrum processes work and the development team can work well. If there are work obstacles, also known as *impediments*, the Scrum Master takes care of their removal. He organizes and moderates Scrum events.
- Development team
  The development team typically consists of 7 +/− 2 members. It is responsible for implementing the user stories planned in a sprint and delivering an increment.

In addition, there are stakeholders outside the Scrum team who have an influence on the project, for example (Fig. 4.5):

Fig. 4.5   Potential
stakeholders in the Scrum
environment

- Customer
  This can be the department in an internal project, in a regular project it can be potential buyers, that is, external customers. The product owner should be in regular contact with the customers.
- User
  These are end users for the product. But it can also be service or operations employees who operate the product, for example within a hotline or service organization, set up users, install security updates, etc.
- Management
  The main task of management is to support the Scrum team, for example with tools and provision of rooms.

4.2.2 Requirements

The capture, maintenance and prioritization of requirements is done in the form of user stories. These are managed as entries in a product backlog, the central working tool in Scrum. The product owner is responsible for the product backlog.

User Stories

A user story focuses on the words *user* and *story*. A user story describes a requirement from the user's perspective as a story. With a user story it is not about a fully formulated specification. What is decisive is a basic understanding of the requirement in the Scrum team. In addition, a user story is a promise to clarify further details as needed. For this, an active role of the product owner is required.

> **User Story**
> Short, simple description of a functionality from the customer's or user's perspective.

It typically follows a pattern to capture the motivation of a role in addition to the actual requirement. The template has proven to be:

As *[Role]* I want *[Function]*, to *[Benefit]*.
Example:

User Story 17 "Delete User"

As *Administrator* I want *to delete a user*, to *save administration effort for invalid users*.

More examples can be found, for example, under [3]. What are the expectations for implementing a user story? Acceptance criteria help to concretize requirements. They define conditions under which the implementation of a user story can be agreed. The acceptance criteria can be listed on the back of a user story (see Fig. 4.6).

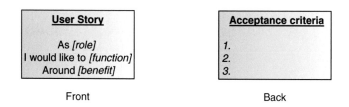

Fig. 4.6 Template for a user story

A user story should be large and comprehensive enough to be implemented in one sprint. If the scope of a story is too great and implementation in one sprint is not possible, it is divided into several smaller user stories. In order not to lose the connection, the original story can be continued as an epic. This is illustrated in Fig. 4.7.

epic Summary of several user stories that belong together content-wise and are developed over several sprints.

Persona

The persona concept, developed by Alan Cooper [6], can help when a product to be developed affects different users and groups of people. The idea is to have a concrete idea of potential users and their abilities in order to better define product properties. Personas as representatives of certain user groups are described as concretely as possible, for example:

- Antonia Müller, 34 years old, married, 3 children, in the company for 12 years, currently responsible for system administration.
- Hacib Jan, 62 years old, single, in partial retirement.

The user stories are then assigned to the representatives of certain user groups. Illustrated with a concrete application case using the example given above:

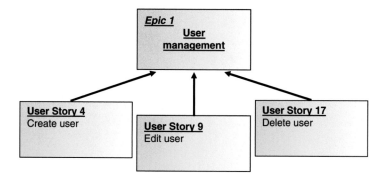

Fig. 4.7 Example of an epic

User Story 17 "Delete User"

As *Administrator* I want to *delete a user* in order to *have a consistent data basis.*

Antonia Müller receives information from the HR department that Hacib Jan has left the company. She wants to delete the user from the system.

Acceptance criteria:

1. After Antonia Müller deleted the user in the system, Hacib Jan receives the error message "User not found" when trying to log in.
2. After Antonia Müller deleted the user in the system, she receives the information "User not in system" when searching for "Hacib Jan" in the database.

Product Backlog

The product backlog is a collection of requirements, such as new or changed functionality, improvements or bug fixes, that should be implemented in the project.

The product owner is responsible for the product backlog (Fig. 4.8). He adds, details, changes, prioritizes and deletes stories as they become relevant. When is a user story ready to be added to the product backlog? It is useful to keep in mind the INVEST model [21] (see Sect. 2.1.3, page 12). It is important that each entry is clearly and understandably formulated as a requirement. Otherwise, it may happen that the product owner is presented with an implemented user story that does not meet his expectations at all. The "Definition of Ready" can be helpful here.

> **Definition of Ready**
> A common understanding within a Scrum team of when a product backlog entry is sufficiently formulated to be transferred to a sprint backlog during a sprint planning [19].

Fig. 4.8 Product owner and product backlog

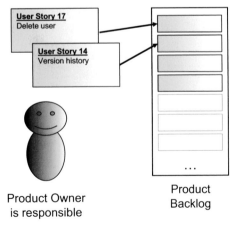

User Story 17
Delete user

User Story 14
Version history

Product Owner
is responsible

Product
Backlog

A checklist for the "Definition of Ready" could include:

- Are the heading and a short description available?
- Is the role described, who benefits from the requirement?
- Is there a concrete example?
- Are the acceptance criteria fully formulated?

The product backlog evolves over the course of the project. Typically, the highest priority entries are the most detailed and clearly described, as they are candidates for the sprint backlog. The lower the priority, the lower the quality of the requirements, as the likelihood of change for these entries is high.

Backlog Refinement
The Backlog Refinement (also called Backlog Grooming) is used to review and revise the entries in the product backlog. The scope is shown in Fig. 4.9. The backlog refinement is a continuous process between the product owner and the development team. Stakeholders can provide valuable support here. It is recommended to schedule one hour per week for this.

4.2.3   Sprint Planning

After each sprint, an increment, a potentially usable software with a defined scope of functions, is delivered.

The goal of a sprint planning is to agree between the product owner and the development team how many and which user stories will be implemented in the next sprint in which order. For this, the product owner prioritizes the entries in the product backlog. Each entry stands for a new or changed functionality in the form of a user story. The length of the sprint planning is calculated as 2 h per sprint week. This results in

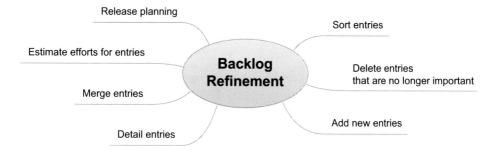

Fig. 4.9   Scope of the backlog refinement

- 4 h for a 2-week sprint,
- 8 h for a 4-week sprint.

Sprint Planning Part 1: What?
The goal of the first part of the sprint planning is to determine the scope of work for the next sprint, the sprint backlog. This means that the sprint backlog contains the entries from the product backlog that will be processed in the next sprint.

As shown in Fig. 4.10, the product owner selects the stories to be implemented, the development team estimates the effort required. The following procedure is recommended:

1. Determine the capacity of the development team
   First, the available capacity is determined, preferably based on the availability of each individual team member. Vacation and sick days, planned absences, training, deployment in other projects, etc., are deducted. In addition, a certain percentage can be deducted, for example for additional effort through refactoring. A flat buffer, for example for unplanned absences, can also be used. The result is the net total person days available for the implementation of backlog entries.
   Example:
   70 person days
   – 10% meetings
   – 10% internal coordination
   56 person days (net)

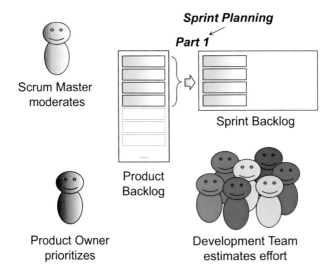

Fig. 4.10 Sprint planning part 1: Determining the user stories

2. Introduce entries from the product backlog

The product owner introduces the user stories to be implemented from the product backlog. He starts with the first, highest-priority entry and explains the user story, gives background information and describes the expectations using acceptance criteria. Questions from the development team are answered. To determine whether a user story is sufficiently understandable, the question "How will the story be demonstrated later?" can help. The clearer the answer, the more sufficient the description of the story [10].

3. Estimate implementation effort

Under the moderation of the Scrum master, the development team estimates the implementation effort for the user story presented. Planning poker has proven itself for this. Planning poker cards or a Planning poker app are used for this. Each project member has the same set of cards or uses the same app. The values shown correspond to story points, the duration of which is defined by the team. Here we assume that one story point corresponds to one hour. Typically, numbers from the Fibonacci sequence are used, ie 1, 2, 3, 5, 8, 13, 21, 34, 55, 89.

The larger intervals at higher numbers indicate the uncertainty associated with the estimate. A '?' Card indicates that you cannot make an estimate. After presenting the user story, each team member thinks of an estimate of the implementation effort. As soon as everyone is ready, all values are revealed and compared at the same time. If there are differences in the estimates, an exchange and another estimation round take place. The goal is to determine an estimated value at the end that is carried by everyone. An example of a first estimation round is shown in Fig. 4.11.

It has proven useful to round off the estimated effort to whole person days. For example: 13 points result in 2 person days of effort.

4. Filling the sprint backlog

The estimated costs are subtracted from the available capacity.

Example: 56 person days – 2 person days = 54 person days.

Then the product owner presents the next story. Step by step, the sprint backlog is filled with stories that are to be implemented in the next sprint until the capacity is used up. The size of the user stories should be chosen so that about 5 to 15 user stories can be implemented in one sprint [10].

In this context, it may turn out that initial work could be done for one or more user stories, but it is clear that no complete implementation is possible. These can be considered as "stretched objectives" in the sprint. This means that they can be worked on, but they are not part of the sprint goal.

5. Defining the sprint goal

Based on the user stories to be implemented, the sprint goal is defined. The sprint goal is a concise, easily understandable summary of all sprint backlog entries. The sprint goal should be achieved by implementing the agreed user stories. It makes it clear to the development team why the increment is created.

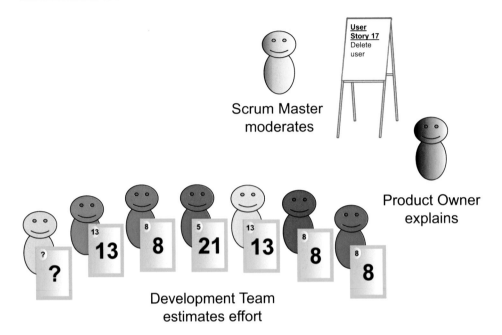

Fig. 4.11 Example of the use of planning poker

6. Commitment
   Based on the sprint goal, the development team provides feedback on the agreement, this is called *commitment*. Is the team convinced that the sprint goal will be achieved? The "5-finger feedback" is proposed with the following meaning:
   - 5 fingers: completely convinced.
   - …
   - 1 finger: not convinced.

   All developers show a hand with 1 to 5 fingers at the same time. If not all developers show 4 or 5 fingers, those who show less than 4 fingers should be asked for their reasons. There is still the possibility to adjust the sprint goal in order to achieve the consent of the development team.

Sprint Planning Part 2: How?

The goal of the second part of the sprint planning is to identify tasks that need to be completed in order to implement the user stories. As shown in Fig. 4.12, the development team derives these tasks from each user story. This is typically done in smaller groups within the development team. Technical aspects such as further development of the architecture, data structures or interface design are discussed. The product owner helps the development team, for example by answering questions. In the end, the sprint backlog with all user stories to be implemented and the associated tasks is defined .

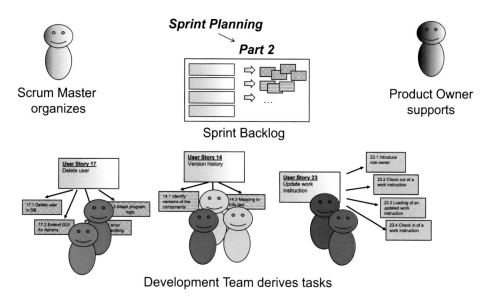

Fig. 4.12 Sprint planning part 2: Deriving tasks

4.2.4 Sprint

A central part of Scrum is the **sprint**. The duration of a sprint is fixed. Usually these are two weeks,[1] but depending on the project, they can also be between one and six weeks. The sprint backlog, defined in the sprint planning, is the basis for the sprint. The goal of a sprint is to create an increment, usable software .

> **Increment**
> The increment is the result of all product backlog entries completed in a sprint and the result of the increments of all previous sprints [19].

The user stories agreed upon in the sprint planning are processed and completed. The question of when a user story or an increment is finished is answered by the "Definition of Done".

---

[1] 60% of respondents in a study said a sprint length of two weeks [11, slide 91].

Definition of Done
Common understanding within a Scrum team of when a product backlog item or product increment is done (according to [19]).

The "Definition of Done" is dependent on the project context and differs from Scrum team to Scrum team. Often there is a checklist. It could, for example, contain the following criteria:

- Code was created in pair programming or checked by another programmer.
- The component tests were carried out and documented.
- The system documentation was extended or adapted.

In some projects there are also two definitions of the "Definition of Done", for example:

- Definition of Done 1
  A story is ready for the Sprint Review and all criteria of the checklist are met.
- Definition of Done 2
  A story was presented in the Sprint Review and accepted. All defined tests for the story were successfully carried out in a specific (test) environment, there are no open errors.
  It should be noted that the "Definition of Done" created by the Scrum team serves as a guideline and should not be considered too formal. The creation of a concept certainly requires other completion criteria than the comprehensive implementation of a complex functionality. Usually the "Definition of Done" develops further during the project.

Task Board
The task board reflects the current state of work in the sprint. It contains the stories to be implemented in priority order, which are defined in the current sprint backlog, as well as the associated tasks. Initially, all tasks are in the "Planned" status (Fig. 4.13, left) .

The task board shows the progress of each task. During the sprint, the tasks move from left to right, first in the "In Progress" status, then in the "Done" status (Fig. 4.13, middle). The goal is that all tasks are finished at the end (Fig. 4.13, right). If all tasks are done, the user story is implemented, provided the "Definition of Done" is met. The task board is best updated regularly during the daily scrum.

Daily Scrum
Typically, the Daily Scrum takes place standing and does not last longer than 15 min. It should take place daily at a fixed time. An overview is shown in Fig. 4.14.

Each team member reports on the status of his work in relation to the sprint goal, preferably directly on the basis of the user stories and tasks listed in the task board:

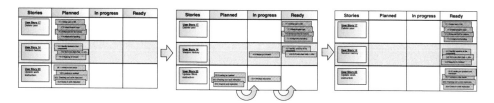

Fig. 4.13   Task board lifecycle

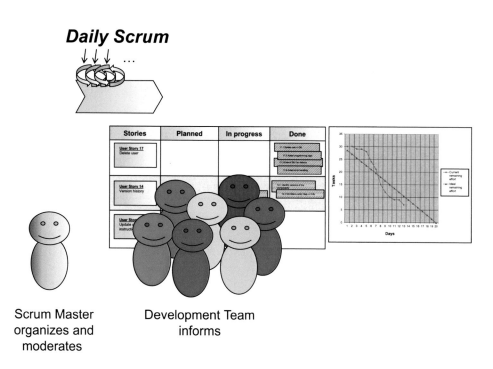

Fig. 4.14   Daily Scrum

1. What have I done to achieve the sprint goal?
2. What do I plan to do to achieve the sprint goal?
3. Are there any obstacles that prevent me from working?

The daily Scrum serves the exchange and mutual support, not the solution of problems. The Scrum master takes care of the removal of the impediments pointed out.

Burndown Chart

The Burndown chart is a visualization of the current work progress. Within a sprint, it represents the remaining work still necessary to achieve the sprint goal.

In the example in Fig. 4.15 the horizontal axis shows the number of days – here 20 working days for a regular 4-week sprint. In the vertical axis is the remaining effort. In the example, the number of tasks is listed, instead of days or hours .

Collection of Work Obstacles

A collection of work obstacles, also referred to as *impediment backlog* or *Scrum* impediment) contains the obstacles to be eliminated by the development team. This collection can be kept in the form of a list, similar to a task list (template in Sect. 6.2). It is also possible to keep the work obstacles and the corresponding status on the task board. The Scrum master is responsible for eliminating the work obstacles as quickly as possible .

4.2.5   Sprint Review

The sprint review is the highlight at the end of a sprint. In addition to the Scrum team, stakeholders are also invited to present the work results (Fig. 4.16). The duration of the sprint review corresponds to one hour per sprint week, so

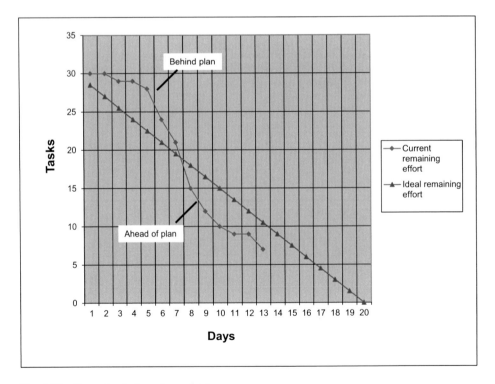

Fig. 4.15   Example of a burndown chart

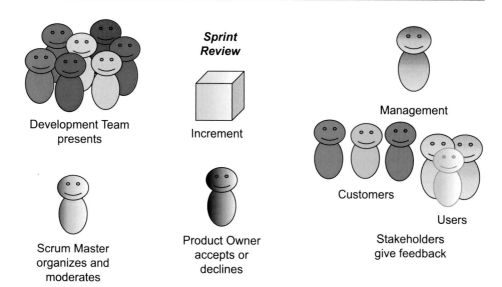

Fig. 4.16 Overview sprint review

- 2 h for a sprint duration of 2 weeks,
- 4 h for a sprint duration of 4 weeks.

The development team presents the work results based on the finished usable product status. This includes all backlog items that were implemented in the sprint. The prerequisite is that they meet the "Definition of Done". The product owner decides on the acceptance of the presented user stories based on the acceptance criteria. Stakeholders give their feedback, which can be incorporated into the planning of the next sprint.

4.2.6 Sprint Retrospective

After a sprint review, a look is taken at the team's work process with the sprint retrospective. It is intended for the development team, as shown in Fig. 4.17. Stakeholders can participate if they are invited. The duration should be 45 min. per sprint week.

The team decides which previous activities to continue or stop and which improvement measures to implement. The goal is continuous process improvement. The following questions have proven to be useful:

1. What went well?
   Whatever has proven effective should be continued.

Fig. 4.17 Overview sprint retrospective

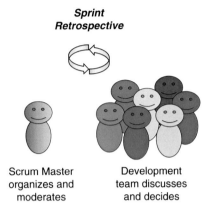

Sprint Retrospective

Scrum Master organizes and moderates

Development team discusses and decides

2. What went wrong?

   Here the team should discuss what should be discontinued or what can be changed. Identified work obstacles are assigned to the Scrum Master.

3. What do we want to improve?

   The team can collect suggestions for improvement and decide together which measures should be implemented concretely.

The first two questions deal with the past, the third with the future. The suggestions for improvement are prioritized by the team. One possibility is that each team member receives three points and can distribute them arbitrarily. In the end, a overall picture results. Fig. 4.18 shows an example.

ID	What do we want to improve?	Prioritization
1	Daily Scrum should start in time	○○○○○
2	Document decisions	○○
3	Create decision templates before customer appointment	○○
4	No phone calls during meetings	○○○
5	Everyone can work two hours a day without outside interference	○○○
6	No detailed discussions in the Daily Scrum	○○
7	We have lunch together on Thursdays	○○
8	Every meeting should have an agenda	○○○○○
9		
10		

Fig. 4.18 Prioritizing improvement measures

4.3   Using Agile Methods

"A good end also requires a good beginning."

Confucius (probably 551–479 BC) This section looks at the use of agile techniques and methods. The introduction of agile approaches depends on the technology and the project environment.

4.3.1   Use in Traditional Projects

The following examples show how certain agile techniques can also be introduced in traditional projects in order to improve communication and collaboration and also to increase the likelihood of success of the project. Agile techniques should be checked and, if expected to be of benefit to the project, gradually introduced in agreement with the project team, possibly on a trial basis. If they are not successful, they can be reversed.

- Daily communication
  Similar to the daily Scrum, the project members meet daily at a fixed time for a short exchange of 15 min. Each project member gives feedback on his or her current work with regard to the next target to be achieved:
  1. What have I done since the last meeting?
  2. What do I plan to do until the next meeting?
  3. What difficulties do I have? Where do I need support?
  This provides an opportunity for those in charge to address problems early and, if possible, to resolve them quickly.
- Work in pairs
  Similar to pair programming in XP, two person teams can be formed to intensively deal with a topic as a pair. One person works, the other observes, comments and asks questions. After a certain time, a role reversal takes place. A better understanding of the topic complex and a higher quality of the developed solution are to be expected.
- Lessons Learned
  An exchange in the project on the current work process can help to address difficulties in the project and to look for solutions and improvements together. You can lean on the retrospective here.
- Regular demonstration
  Up-to-date interim results can be requested and shown at milestone dates, analogous to the sprint review. Stakeholders can also be invited to these presentations. Their feedback can be used by the client, for example, to identify change requirements before the project is completed.

4.3.2 Introduction of Agile Processes

The introduction of an agile overall approach such as Scrum is significantly more complex and challenging than introducing individual agile techniques. If the use of Scrum or a similar approach is planned, a collaboration model should be defined and implemented as quickly as possible with regular iterations. First of all, one should acquire knowledge about Scrum, for example from the Scrum guide [19], specialist literature [8, 10], certification seminars (see Sect. 5.1), workshops or seminars.

Next, the contractual or employment relationship between the project participants should be clarified. According to Josef Willkommer [22], it is recommended to create an initial backlog with requirements at a high level of abstraction together with the customer. Based on this, a rough effort estimation is carried out. For this, the number of sprints required is multiplied by the number of team members available and the corresponding daily or hourly rates. Then the client can decide, for example, on a budget limit. A limited project initiation or a sprint 0 can then be planned to introduce Scrum and then start with regular sprints.

4.4 Hybrid Process Models

"You have to learn from the old to make the new."
Berthold Brecht (1898–1956) Hybrid approaches stand for the combination of different methods. In a study, 43% of participants said they were working on a mixed form, using both classical and agile development processes [11, slide 13].

Hybrid project management can take many forms, for example the embedding of Scrum in a classical approach. This is especially common in global integration projects when, for example, different suppliers and teams deliver solutions or sub-products for the development of a complex overall product and then these are brought together. This is a typical approach in the automotive industry in the development of new vehicles, in mechanical engineering in the construction of complex machines or in the media environment in the design of innovative services. Depending on the type of commissioning, suppliers or project partners use different methods. Often it is not possible to implement a uniform procedure. The challenge is then to coordinate these different methods, to bring together the work results and to obtain a functioning end product. For the resulting "forced" hybrid project management, when different teams work with different methods, the following strategies are recommended:

- Specification and development against interfaces
  This is particularly useful in IT projects. First, the interfaces between individual components or subsystems are defined. A schema specifies the semantics of exchanged data. Concrete examples increase understanding. If these are agreed, the development partners can develop against these interfaces. As long as the development is not com-

plete, simulations can be used. The procedure can also be used for the development of embedded systems, for example in control unit development.

- Early integration with a minimal product
  The more risky the integration, the more it makes sense to bring the integration forward with a minimal product. For this purpose, the minimal product is defined and all project partners focus on the development of the functionality required for this. A temporal consolidation takes place via milestones. There is joint planning and regular integration with testing.

An example of a targeted hybrid approach is the combination of the V-model (see page 7) with agile, iterative elements for the development of mechatronic systems [7, pages 14–22].

4.5   Limits of Agility

The use of agile methods increases the likelihood of successful projects [9]. However, they are not a panacea. If an agile project fails, it should not be judged too quickly. Among other things, the use of agile methods should be checked and it should not be assumed that the responsible persons have applied the methods used incorrectly.

For example, Bertrand Meyer deals critically with the enthusiasm for agile methods [14]. Agile methods do not include a strategy phase for preliminary work (compare Sect. 3.1). This makes it more difficult to carry out a comprehensive requirements analysis in complex projects and to design a solid architecture in IT projects, which can lead to quality problems. There is also the risk that documentation will be neglected, which will lead to limited maintainability. This can be countered by, for example, each user story containing the standard acceptance criterion "Adaptation of the system documentation" as a standard. This makes it possible to check whether the user story implemented has also been sufficiently documented for operation, for example in a system administration manual.

The organization of tests in agile IT projects is also challenging [10]. On the one hand, it may be claimed that a requirement will be completely tested and handed over. On the other hand, it is possible that the implementation is carried out with developer tests and customer tests are carried out after delivery (see "Definition of Done" on page 140). In both cases, the procedures have to be organized and coordinated in the project.

4.6   Summary

Agile methods and techniques are used by numerous companies and organizations. The main reasons for this are accelerated software development, the ability to change priorities and increased productivity.

Many of the twelve practices originally defined for XP can be found in other agile processes, such as test-driven software development, short release cycles with continuous regular integration, programming in pairs and refactoring to keep projects "healthy".

Scrum is a framework for lean software development and the most used agile method. Its greatest advantage is that a usable product is available after each sprint: the increment. Three roles are defined: the product owner, the scrum master and the development team with seven +/− two members. The product backlog contains and prioritizes the requirements. Scrum is characterized by the timebox approach, the sprint and all other events are time-limited: the sprint planning, the sprint, the daily scrum, the sprint review and the sprint retrospective. The scrum master as a "servant leader" is responsible for the development team to work well and obstacles to be removed.

The use of agile methods can be done step by step, even during the execution of a project with a classical approach. If a project is to be carried out in a completely agile way, contract and employment relationships should be clarified in advance. To minimize the risk, it is recommended to have a limited agile collaboration on a trial basis to then clarify the further procedure.

Hybrid approaches arise in practice when different project teams work together and thus different approaches are used. The common approach should be agreed upon by the responsible parties at an early stage.

Agile methods are also criticized in part and should therefore not be used indiscriminately. Before using agile techniques, it is recommended to check in each case whether they are really helpful for the specific project.

4.7   Problems

4.1 Reasons What are the reasons for using agile methods in projects?

4.2 Differences How do classical and agile development models differ?

4.3 XP Explain the XP practice system metaphor.

4.4 Scrum How is Scrum defined?

4.5 Stakeholders in the Scrum environment Name and describe roles that can influence a Scrum project as stakeholders.

4.6 Product Backlog What does a product backlog contain and who is responsible for it?

4.7 Roles in Scrum What roles does Scrum have and what are their characteristics?

4.8 Scrum Events

(a) What events are there in Scrum?

(b) Which of the events in Scrum are timeboxed and what are the guidelines?

4.9 Scrum Artifacts Name the artifacts in Scrum.

4.10 Merging What strategies are there for integrating project results when project teams use both sequential and agile approaches within a project?

4.11 Acceptance What are the differences in project acceptance in the sequential and agile environment?

References

1. Beck, K.: Extreme programming explained: Embrace Change, 2. ed. Addison-Wesley (2000)
2. Beedle, M., von Bennekum, A., Cockburn, A., et al.: Manifest für Agile Softwareentwicklung (2020). https://agilemanifesto.org/iso/de/manifesto.html. Accessed: 23 Aug 2022
3. Cohn, M.: User Stories and User Story Examples. Mountain Goat Software (2020). https://www.mountaingoatsoftware.com/agile/user-stories. Accessed: 23 Aug 2022
4. CollabNet VersionOne: 13th annual State of Agile Report (2022). https://stateofagile.com. Accessed: 23 Aug 2022
5. Collier, K.W.: Agile Analytics: A Value-Driven Approach to Business Intelligence and Data Warehousing: Delivering the Promise of Business Intelligence. Addison-Wesley Professional (2011)
6. Cooper, A.: The Inmates Are Running the Asylum. Sams Publishing (2004)
7. Feldmüller, D., Sticherling, N.: Agile Methoden in der Entwicklung mechatronischer Produkte. projektMANAGEMENT aktuell (2016)
8. Gloger, B.: Scrum: Produkte zuverlässig und schnell entwickeln. Carl Hanser Verlag (2016)
9. Hastie, S., Wojewoda, S.: Standish Group 2015 Chaos Report – Q&A with Jennifer Lynch on Oct 04, 2015 (2015). https://www.infoq.com/articles/standish-chaos-2015/. Accessed: 23 Aug 2022
10. Kniberg, H.: Scrum und XP Feldbericht – Wie wir das mit Scrum machen. C4media (2015). https://www.infoq.com/minibooks/scrum-xp-from-the-trenches-2/. Accessed: 23 Aug 2022
11. Komus, A., et al.: Studie Status Quo (Scaled) Agile 2019/2020. BPM-Labor für Business Process Management und Organizational Excellence, Hochschule Koblenz University of Applied Science (2020). https://www.process-and-project.net/studien/studienunterseiten/status-quo-scaled-agile-2020/. Accessed: 23 Aug 2022
12. Leopold, K., Kaltenecker, S.: Kanban in der IT: Eine Kultur der kontinuierlichen Verbesserung schaffen, 2. Auflage. Carl Hanser Verlag (2013)
13. Lindner, D., Ott, M., Leyh, C.: Der digitale Arbeitsplatz – KMU zwischen Tradition und Wandel. HMD Praxis der Wirtschaftsinformatik (2017). https://agile-unternehmen.de/was-ist-agil-definition/. Accessed: 1. Aug. 2020
14. Meyer, B.: Agile! The Good, the Hype and the Ugly. Springer International Publishing (2014)
15. Ohno, T.: Toyota Production System – Beyond Large-Scale Production. Productivity Press, Cambridge Massachusetts (1988)

16. Reddy, A.: The scrumban [R]Evolution: Getting the most out of agile, scrum, and lean kanban. Addison-Wesley Professional (2015)
17. Ries, E.: The Lean Startup: How Today's Entrepreneurs Use Continuous Innovation to Create Radically Successful Businesses. Crown Business (2011)
18. Schwaber, K.: Scrum Development Process. In: J. Sutherland, D. Patel, C. Casanave, J. Miller, G. Hollowell (eds.) OOPSLA Business Object Design and Implementation Workshop. London: Springer (1997)
19. Schwaber, K., Sutherland, J.: The Scrum Guide (2020). https://www.scrumguides.org/scrum-guide.html. Accessed: 23 Aug 2022
20. The Standish Group: Chaos Manifesto – The Laws of CHAOS and the CHAOS 100 Best PM Practices (2011)
21. Wake, B.: INVEST in Good Stories, and SMART Tasks (2003). https://xp123.com/articles/invest-in-good-stories-and-smart-tasks/. Accessed: 23 Aug 2022
22. Willkommer, J.: Modernes (Projekt-)Management, Scrum, Kanban, Management 3.0 & Co (2017). https://www.techdivision.com/lp/projektmanagement-whitepaper.html. Accessed: 23 Aug 2022
23. Wolf, M., Büning, N., Schmahl, H., Cramer, M.: Studie zur Agilität in Unternehmen – Demystifizierung von Agilität. FH Aachen, Korn Ferry, Inititative Deutschland Digital, neuland (2018). https://karlheinzland.com/downloads/Studie_agilitaet_2018.pdf. Accessed: 23 Aug 2022

Outlook

5

This chapter gives you an overview of certification options in project management. It provides a glimpse into the future of project management and introduces you to ways in which you can become more involved with the subject. Glossaries of project management terms can be found in [3 or 1].

5.1 Certifications

It is possible to become certified by different organizations in project management and Scrum. Here is a selection.

- Certificates from the German Association for Project Management (GPM) [6]:
  - Basic Project Management Certificate (GPM)
  - Certified Project Management Associate (IPMA® Level D)
  - Certified Project Manager (IPMA® Level C)
  - Certified Senior Project Manager (IPMA® Level B)
  - Certified Project Director (IPMA® Level A)
- PMI certificates (extract) [7]:
  - Certified Associate in Project Management (CAPM ®)
  - Project Management Professional (PMP ®)
  - Program Management Professional (PgMP ®)
  In addition, certificates are offered for other topics, such as agility.
- PRINCE2 certificates [4]
  - PRINCE2 Foundation Examination
  - PRINCE2 Practitioner Examination
  - PRINCE2 Agile Practitioner Examination

© Springer-Verlag GmbH Germany, part of Springer Nature 2022
D. Alam and U. Gühl, *Project Management for Practice*,
https://doi.org/10.1007/978-3-662-65159-9_5

- Certificate of the Working Group Software Quality and advanced Training (German: Arbeitskreis Software-Qualität und -Fortbildung e. V. (ASQF)) [2]
  The ASQF offers a certification to the ASQF® Certified Professional for Project Management (CPPM).
- Scrum certificates from Scrum.org [9]:
  - Professional Scrum Master™ in three levels PSM I, PSM II and PSM III
  - Professional Scrum Product Owner™ in three levels PSPO I, PSPO II and PSPO III
  - Professional Scrum Developer™
- Scrum certificates from the Scrum Alliance [8]:
  - Certified ScrumMaster®
  - Advanced Certified ScrumMaster
  - Certified Scrum Professional®-ScrumMaster
  - Certified Scrum Product Owner®
  - Advanced Certified Scrum Product Owner
  - Certified Scrum Professional®-Product Owner
  - Certified Scrum Developer®
  - Certified Scrum Professional®

5.2   Project Management in the Future

In software development, the agile approach is increasingly gaining ground. According to CollabNet VersionOne in 2018, 97% of companies used agile processes [5]. In the future, agile project management will take up more space. Individual methods and innovative ideas such as timeboxing (see milestone planning in Sect. 3.3.3) or the retrospective from Scrum (see Sect. 4.2.6) will be found more and more in non-IT project management in the future.

5.3   ...and What Else we Want to Give You

We would like to repeat the most important findings for us in a summary:

- Make those affected into participants.
- Demand truth and commitment.
- Allow failure in time.
- Include project employees in effort estimates.
- Let the right people do the tasks that are right for them.
- Consider environmental aspects

Projects necessarily also affect and shape the environment. Take responsibility for ensuring that projects change the environment positively, in the worst case as little disadvantageously as possible. Consider environmental protection in projects that deal with the creation of products or in which waste is generated. Consider resource conservation and recycling with a holistic approach at an early stage.

In conclusion, we strongly recommend that you also train in social and emotional competence, communication and conflict management for a successful project management. Use regular exchanges with experts, use supervision and peer consultation.

The authors wish you the best of luck for your projects!

5.4 Summary

Certification programs of national and international organizations provide the opportunity to expand and confirm knowledge in project management. There are often also specific qualification programs within companies. In the future, agile project management will play an increasingly important role.

References

1. Angermeier, G.: Projektmagazin Projektmanagement-Glossar (2020). https://www.projektmagazin.de/glossarterm. Accessed: 23. Aug 2022
2. ASQF: ASQF® Certified Professional for Project Management (CPPM) (2020). https://www.asqf.de/asqf/produkte/asqf-certified-professional-for-project-management-cppm/. Accessed: 23 Aug 2022
3. Axelos: PRINCE2® 2017 glossary of terms (2020). https://www.axelos.com/glossaries-of-terms. Accessed: 1 Aug 2020
4. Axelos: PRINCE2® Certification — Qualifications & Exams (2020). https://www.axelos.com/certifications/prince2. Accessed: 23 Aug 2022
5. CollabNet VersionOne: 13th annual State of Agile Report (2019). https://stateofagile.com. Accessed: 23 Aug 2022
6. GPM Deutsche Gesellschaft für Projektmanagement e. V.: Zertifizierung (2020). https://www.gpm-ipma.de/zertifizierung.html. Accessed: 23 Aug 2022
7. Project Management Institute: Certifications (2020). https://www.pmi.org/certifications. Accessed: 23 Aug 2022
8. Scrum Alliance: Certifications by scrum team Role (2020). https://www.scrumalliance.org/get-certified. Accessed: 23 Aug 2022
9. Scrum.org: Professional Scrum™ Certifications (2020). https://www.scrum.org/professional-scrum-certifications. Accessed: 23 Aug 2022

Templates

As shown in Fig. 6.1, you will find the following templates for the project phases:

- Cross-sectional topics
  - Project profile (page 157)
  - Task list (page 158)
  - Requirements list (page 160)
  - Project handbook (page 161)
  - Risk list (page 169)
  - Communication plan (page 170)
  - Minutes (page 171)
- Strategy phase
  - RACI matrix (page 172)
  - Environmental analysis (page 173)
  - Project order (page 174)
- Planning phase
  - Work breakdown structure (page 175)
  - Work package (page 176)
  - Milestone plan (page 177)
  - Resource plan/Cost schedule (page 178)
- Realization phase
  - Milestone report (page 179)
  - Project status (page 180)
- Closure phase
  - Project closure report (page 181)

© Springer-Verlag GmbH Germany, part of Springer Nature 2022
D. Alam and U. Gühl, *Project Management for Practice*,
https://doi.org/10.1007/978-3-662-65159-9_6

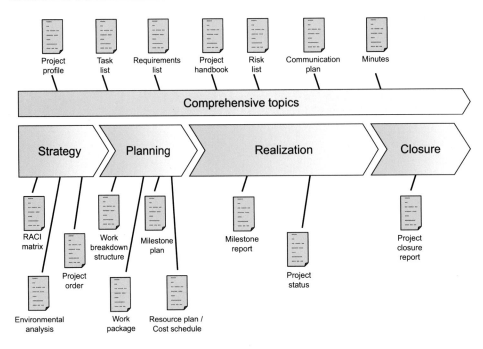

Fig. 6.1   Templates assigned to project phases

Project profile

Project name		Project no.	
Principal			
Project manager			
Version/Date		Status	

Steering committee	
Project team	
Stakeholder	
Supplier	

Project start		Project end	

Objectives	
Project scope	
Milestones	
Payment agreements	

_____   _____   _____
Place, date   Principal   Project manager

Task list

Project name	<Name of project>	Project no.	<Number of project>
Responsible	<Name of responsible>		
Version/Date	<0.1 / Day.Month.Year>		

No.	Task	Category	Respon-sible	Start date	Due date	Prio-rity	Status	Result	Comments
<Id>	<Headline of task>	<Class of task>	<Name of res-ponsible>	<Start date of task>	<until when to finish>	<e. g. high, mediu m, low>	<e. g. open, in progress , done>	<Descri ption of result>	<Remarks with date and initials>

Task list

Project name			Project no.	
Responsible				
Version/Date				

No.	Task	Category	Respon-sible	Start date	Due date	Prio-rity	Status	Result	Comments

Requirements list

Project name		Project no.	
Responsible			
Version/Date			

No.	Requirement	Justification	Responsible	Priority	Status	Comments

Project manual

Project:	....
Author:	....
Version:	....
Last saved:	....
Location:	....

Document administration

Version history

Date	Author	Version	Content changes

Distribution list

Date	Version	Distributors, names

Approval

Date	Version	Distributors, names

Related documents

Author, title	Version	Location

Project manual

1   Introduction

1.1 Purpose

1.2 Short description of the project

1.3 Contact persons

Name	Role	Department	Phone	E-mail

Project manual

2   Project overview

....

2.1 Situation analysis

....
....
....
....

2.2 Environmental analysis

....
....
....
....

2.3 Project order

....
....
....
....

2.4 Objectives

....
....
....
....

Project manual

2.5 Communication

....
....
....
....

2.6 Escalation

....
....
....
....

2.7 Rules

....
....
....
....

2.8 Documentation

....
....
....
....

Project manual

3   Project plan

3.1 Work breakdown structure (WBS)

3.2 Work packages

3.3 Time schedule

3.4 Resource plan and cost schedule

Project manual

3.5 Project organization

....
....
....
....

3.6 Kickoff

....
....
....
....

Project manual

4   Project execution

....

4.1 Milestones

....
....
....
....

4.2 Project controlling

....
....
....
....

4.3 Protocols

....
....
....
....

4.4 Risk management

....
....
....
....

Project manual

5   Project closure

....

5.1 Acceptance

....
....
....
....

5.2 Project closure report

....
....
....
....

5.3 Transition

....
....
....
....

Risk list

Project name		Project no.	
Responsible			
Version/Date			

	Risk description				Quantification			Risk mitigation	
No.	Risk identification	Potential cause	Contact person	Date	P	I	Risk = P * I	Status	Actions

Legend:

P = Probability of incidence (of the risk)

    1 = low

    2 = medium

    3 = high

I = Estimated impact (impact on the project if the risk occurs)

    1 = less critical

    2 = critical

    3 = very critical

$Risk$ = Probability P * Estimated impact I

    1 or 2 = low risk

    3 or 4 = medium risk

    6 or 9 = high risk

Communication plan

Project name		Project no.	
Project manager			
Version/Date			
Author			

Type of communication	Who/ With whom	Purpose	Frequency	Comments

Minutes

Project name		Project no.	
Location		Date	
Minute taker		Version	
Subject			

Participants	
Distribution list	

No.	(A)ction Item (D)ecision (I)nformation	Description	Responsible	Due date

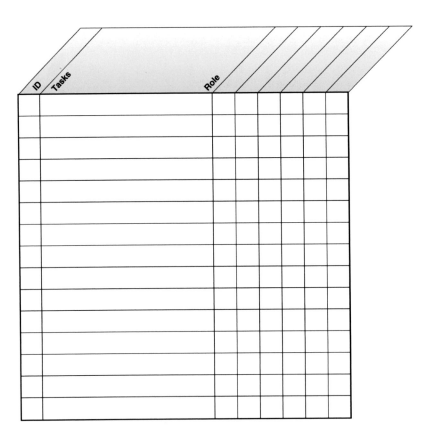

RACI matrix

Project name		Project no.	
Project Manager			
Version/Date			

R = Responsible - responsible for implementation

A = Accountable - legally responsible

C = Consulted - advisory

I = Informed - will be informed

Environmental analysis

Project name		Project no.	
Responsible			
Version/Date		Status	

No.	Stakeholder	Possible role in project	Setting to project	Possible influence/ Power	Measures/Strategies

Project order

Project name		Project no.	
Principal			
Project manager			
Version/Date		Status	

Steering committee	
Project team	

Project start		Project end	

Objectives	
Non-goals	
Project scope	
Milestones	
Contract value	

_____   _____   _____
Place, date   Principal   Project manager

Work breakdown structure (WBS)

Project name		Project no.	
Project manager			
Version/Date		Status	

WBS No.	Subproject/ Work package	Responsible	Plan		Actual	
			Work load	Duration	Work load	Duration

Work package (WP)

Project name		Project no.	
WP name		WP Id	
WP owner			
WP approval			
Version/Date		Status	

Progress control	Plan		Actual	
	Workload	Duration	Workload	Duration
	Start	End	Start	End
Comments				

Objective	
Preconditions (Input)	
Scope	
Results (Output)	

Milestone plan

Project name		Project no.	
Project manager			
Version/Date			
Author			

No.	Planned date	Current date	Milestone	Id	Criterion	Result

Resource/Cost plan

Project name		Project no.	
Project manager			
Version/Date			
Author			

Personnel costs			Plan			Actual		
WBS No.	Working package/ Name	Int. / ext.	Hours	Hourly rate	Costs	Hours	Hourly rate	Costs
Subtotal personal costs								

Material costs			Plan			Actual		
WBS No.	Working package	Item	Quanti ty	Price	Costs	Quanti ty	Price	Costs
Subtotal material costs								
Total								

Milestone report

Project name		Project no.	
Project manager			
Version/Date			
Author			
Milestone		Status	

	Exit criteria			Result		
No.	Criterion	Respon-sible	Accepted by	Description	Status	Comments

Project status

Project name		Project no.	
Project manager			
Report period		Version/Date	
Author			

1. Status

Results	
Activities	

2. Forecast

Planned activities	
Planned activities until end of project (Backlog)	
Risks	
Open points, issues	

Project closure report

Project name		Project no.	
Principal			
Project manager			
Version/Date		Status	
Project start		Project end	
Project results			
Acceptance			
Project evaluation			
• Degree of achievement of objectives			
• Delivered quality			
• Amount of costs			
• Time needed			
Findings			
• Positive impressions			
• Potential for improvement			

Place, date	Principal	Project manager

Solutions

© Springer-Verlag GmbH Germany, part of Springer Nature 2022
D. Alam and U. Gühl, *Project Management for Practice,*
https://doi.org/10.1007/978-3-662-65159-9

Problems from Chap. 1

1.1 Motivation

Why should one deal with the topic of project management?

The proportion of project management activities is increasing in many professions. In the future, more and more project management experts will be needed worldwide.

1.2 Project Definition

(a) What is a project?

A project is a one-time, limited-time undertaking with a beginning and an end.

(b) What are the characteristics of a project?

- Defined goal
- Uniqueness and novelty
- Time-limited
- Resource-limited
- Sufficiently complex
- Cross-sectoral

1.3 Project Management

How is project management defined?

The totality of leadership tasks, organisation, techniques and means for the initiation, definition, planning, control and completion of projects

1.4 Success Factors

Name at least three success factors for projects.

(a) Involving users
(b) Support by top management
(c) Clear requirements
(d) Sensible planning
(e) Realistic expectations

© Springer-Verlag GmbH Germany, part of Springer Nature 2022
D. Alam and U. Gühl, *Project Management for Practice,*
https://doi.org/10.1007/978-3-662-65159-9

(f) Small project milestones
(g) Competent employees
(h) Clear responsibility (ownership)
(i) Clear visions and topics
(j) Hardworking, goal-oriented project team

1.5 Failure

What are the most common reasons for project failure?
(a) Poor communication
(b) Unclear requirements and goals
(c) Problems in the organization

Problems from Chap. 2

2.1 Requirements

What are possible consequences of a non-systematic requirements analysis?

- Significantadditional costs for error correction
- No basis for capturing project progress

2.2 Change Management

(a) What significance and effects do changes have in classical and agile projects?
- Classical projects
  The assumption in classical projects is that after the corresponding phase is complete, the requirements are fully formulated. Classical projects are therefore well suited if the requirements are clear at an early stage and no or only minor changes are expected.
- Agile projects
  At the beginning of each iteration, changes can be addressed and considered in the project. Agile methods support changes as planned and are therefore well suited for projects in which numerous and extensive changes are expected.

(b) Name and explain how changes can be planned and controlled in projects.
- Consideration of a buffer in project planning
  The larger the probability of changes, the larger the buffer should be. This can be used in case of changes. The project manager is responsible for this.
- Introduction of a change management process
  Especially in larger and more complex projects, professional and transparent change management is necessary. It is recommended to appoint a change manager, to define a change process and to establish a body (Change Control Board) for the assessment and decision-making of changes.
- Application of an agile approach model
  With agile methods, changes can be made regularly and targeted in a project.

© Springer-Verlag GmbH Germany, part of Springer Nature 2022
D. Alam and U. Gühl, *Project Management for Practice*,
https://doi.org/10.1007/978-3-662-65159-9

2.3 Project Culture

Name soft soft skills in a project.

- Identification with the project
- Willingness to cooperate internally and externally
- Fairness and respect
- Communication skills
- Conflict management skills
- Activity level for the project
- Openness

2.4 Communication

(a) What is the impact of poor communication in a project?

   Poor communication is the most common reason why a project fails.

(b) How can a project manager improve communication in a project?

- Active listening
- Always approachable
- Lead by example
- Positive attitude towards the project
- Empathy and appreciation of all project participants
- Good manners
- Consistent actions
- Open transparent communication
- Talk to people directly

(c) How do verbal and nonverbal communication differ?

- Verbal communication stands for linguistic content in oral (direct or by telephone) or written form (by e-mail, fax, letter).
- Nonverbal communication stands for non-linguistic content, expressed for example by body language, eye contact, tone of voice, external form or reaction speed.

2.5 Documentation

(a) What role does documentation play in a project?

- Documentation serves mainly for information and as an essential quality criterion for transparency and traceability:
  - Which problem had to be solved (project assignment)?
  - How was the problem solved (project result)?
  - How was the project progress?
     Why was this particular solution chosen, what were the advantages?
     What effort and what costs have arisen?

- The goal is a documentation that is as complete and meaningful as possible, which is best written parallel to the project implementation.

(b) What are the quality aspects of documentation?

- Uniformity
- Systematics
- Traceability
- Completeness
- Rapid availability
- Relevance

2.6 Quality

(a) What does quality mean to you in project management?

Ensuring that the work results correspond to the project objectives. The focus here is on the professional project contents.

(b) How can quality be ensured in a project?

- Define a role quality management
- Development of a learning organization
- Solution-oriented approach to dealing with problems
- Establishing continuous improvement
- Consolidation with project partners
- Conducting reviews
- Use of checklist

2.7 Risk Management

(a) Why should risk management be carried out in a project?

- Risks are a typical feature of a project.
- Risk management helps to deal with risks early on in order to prevent them from occurring or to mitigate the effects of risks that do occur.
- Risk management can be used to identify potential risks and developments in a timely manner and to take appropriate measures to ensure the success of the project.
- Note: Public companies are required to deal with risk management in order to protect shareholders, customers, suppliers and employees.

(b) Is risk management a one-time or an iterative process?

Risk management is an iterative process. In projects there are almost always changes, each change can bring new risks with it.

2.8 Methods

What is a method?

A method describes the way to the goal.

Problems from Chap. 3

3.1 Project Goals
(a) What do you understand by a goal definition?
   Defining the often unclear, too demanding or even contradictory ideas of the initiators of a project as project goals.
(b) Target operationalization: What does a target description include?
   The target description should answer the following questions:
   • What should be achieved?
   • How much should be achieved?
   • When should it be achieved?
   • Where should it be achieved?
(c) Why are project goals important?
   Unclear project goals often lead to the failure of a project.
(d) What should you definitely pay attention to when describing the goals?
   • The goals should be quantifiable: make goals measurable.
   • Define non-goals: What should not be achieved?
(e) Which methods can you use to find project goals?
   • Brainstorming
   • Mind mapping

3.2 Environment analysis
(a) Which methods can you use for the environment analysis?
   • RACI matrix
   • Mind mapping
(b) What are possible problems in the environment analysis?
   • Insufficient information policy leads to missing or incorrect information.
   • Hidden agenda: people affected by the project do not openly express their concerns, objections and expectations.

© Springer-Verlag GmbH Germany, part of Springer Nature 2022
D. Alam and U. Gühl, *Project Management for Practice,*
https://doi.org/10.1007/978-3-662-65159-9

(c) What is the difference between the environment analysis and the risk analysis?
- The environment analysis examines the attitudes of all people who influence the project.
- The risk analysis considers and evaluates (monetarily) potential damage from risks.

3.3 Milestones
(a) What is a milestone?
- An event of special importance
- An intermediate goal with important project results
(b) Why are milestones necessary in a project?
- To check at defined points during project realization whether the planned goals have been achieved or can be achieved.
- Milestones define measurable criteria to approve activities.
- Milestones can be used to divide a project into phases, which supports the targeted joint approach.

3.4 Project Plan
What are the most important plans summarized in the project plan?
Explain these briefly.
- Work Breakdown Structure (WBS)
  The WBS structures a project and thus describes its content and scope.
- Time Schedule
  The time schedule assigns the work packages identified in the WBS to a realistic project course.
- Resource plan and cost schedule
  The resource plan and cost schedule identifies the resources required for processes, work packages and subprojects and represents the costs incurred for the project.

3.5 Work Breakdown Structure (WBS)
(a) Describe the content and purpose of the work breakdown structure.
  The work breakdown structure (WBS) is the basis for the following points:
- Distribution of responsibilities in the project
  - The WBS breaks down the project goal into operational goals for the project members.
  - The WBS allows to clearly delimit the tasks and assign them to the project members.
- Estimation of time and project costs
  - Creating a WBS leads to transparency of the entire scope of work.
  - This transparency is a prerequisite for the estimation of the time and costs required.
- Project control
  - The WBS facilitates early and targeted response to process disruptions, delays, capacity bottlenecks and budget overruns.
  - The WBS also helps with the regular assessment of project risks.

- Structure of the project documentation
  The WBS can be used as a principle of project documentation, reporting and the agenda of project status meetings.
(b) How can a work breakdown structure be created? When should which different procedure be used?
  - Top down—Deductive approach—From the general to the individual
    Starting from the project goal, sub-projects and finally work packages are created. Useful for clear projects.
  - Bottom up—Inductive approach—From the individual to the general
    First, the work packages for the project goal are collected, then the work packages are grouped into the sub-projects. Recommended for projects that are difficult to manage.
(c) Explain how a work breakdown structure can be structured.
  - Function-oriented WBS
    Structuring according to activities with an easier assignment to functional areas.
  - Object-oriented WBS
    Structuring according to all relevant objects or parts of the project
  - Process-oriented WBS
    The representation follows a temporal sequence.
  - Mixed-oriented WBS
    This is a combination of the above-mentioned structuring options.
(d) What advantages does a WBS offer?
  - Assignment of responsibilities
  - Basis of project control
  - Basis of project documentation
  - Risk assessment is easier
  - Basis for estimating project duration and project costs
(e) What are the limits of the WBS?
  - No temporal representation of the sequence of work packages within the project
  - No overview of the utilization of project resources

3.6 Resource plan and cost schedule

What is the benefit of a resource plan and cost schedule?
- It provides transparency by uncovering the flow of payments in the project.
- From the need for resources and financing, which was determined by the effort estimation for work packages, processes and projects, the total project costs can be extrapolated.

3.7 Project organization

(a) List the organization forms you know.
  - Pure functional project organization (by areas, departments)
  - Functional project organization

- Matrix project organization
- Pure project organization
- Project society

(b) What questions should a project organization chart answer?
- Who is the principal?
- Who is the project manager? Who are the subproject managers? Who are the people responsible for the work packages?
- Who accepts what results?

3.8 Project organization—Assessment

(a) Is a line organization suitable for carrying out a project?

A line organization is usually not suitable for carrying out projects. Reason: Existing line organizations are
- ideal for fulfilling regularly recurring known (mostly department-oriented) business transactions
- not flexible enough for a quick reaction to problems and change requirements

(b) What are the advantages of a project organization?
- There is a clear leadership responsibility and decision-making competence of the project manager for effective project implementation.
- A high level of identification of the project team with the project is possible.
- Conflicts do not have to be fought out over the hierarchies of the line organization.

3.9 Project controlling

(a) Whatdo you understand by project controlling?

The aim of project controlling is to keep the actual project course as closely in line with the planned project course as possible in terms of costs, deadlines and results.

(b) What does project controlling require and what does it include?

The basis for determining the target-performance comparison is the project plan. The actual situation arises from current project information. This makes it possible to compare planned and actual: Deviations can be detected and analyzed. Control measures are derived from this in order to correct any planned-actual deviations that may exist.

3.10 Traffic Light Logic

Explain how traffic light logic can be used in status reports.

Traffic light logic provides a quick overview of the status of a project, subproject or work package. The following interpretation of the traffic light colors has proven to be effective:

- green: on schedule.
- yellow: deviation from plan, but controllable by measures of the responsible person.

- red: deviation from plan, no longer controllable by measures of the responsible person, support required.

3.11 Closure Phase

Whyis the project acceptance closely linked to change management?

The project acceptance can require extensive activities if many deficiencies have been found. These activities, according to the specified change process, are to be

- planned,
- eliminated, and
- post-control.

Problems from Chap. 4

4.1 Reasons
What are the reasons for using agile methods in projects?

- Shorter product introduction time,
- Optimization of quality,
- Reduction of project risks.

4.2 Differences
How do classical and agile development models differ?
- Classical approaches are characterized by a sequential processing of phases with a relatively extensive planning phase that extends over the entire project. Agile approaches work with iterations, each of which ends with a potentially deliverable product. Here the scope of a project is variable, a detailed planning is only provided for one iteration.
- In classical approaches, the customer is typically only involved in late phases. In agile approaches there is a constant communication with the customer.
- In classical approaches there is a hierarchical organizational structure, in agile approaches the team is in the foreground, which is provided with all means for a successful work by the management.

4.3 XP
Explain the XP practice system metaphor.

A system metaphor is an architectural guideline for communication within the team and with the customer. It stands for a vision of how the system should work.

4.4 Scrum
How is Scrum defined?

Scrum is a framework within which defined processes and techniques can be used. In Scrum there are roles, events, artifacts and rules that link them together.

© Springer-Verlag GmbH Germany, part of Springer Nature 2022
D. Alam and U. Gühl, *Project Management for Practice,*
https://doi.org/10.1007/978-3-662-65159-9

4.5 Stakeholders in the Scrum Environment

Name and describe roles that can influence a Scrum project as stakeholders.

- Customers
  This can for example be a department or potential buyers of the product to be created.
- Users
  This can be both end users who use the product and operational staff who support the product.
- Management
  The main task of management is to support the Scrum team.

4.6 Product Backlog

What does a product backlog contain and who is responsible for it?

The product backlog contains requirements, sorted by priority. The product owner is responsible for the product backlog.

4.7 Roles in Scrum

What roles does Scrum know and what are their characteristics?

- Product owner
  He is responsible for formulating and prioritizing the requirements in the product backlog and representing the customer.
- Development team
  It is responsible for developing the product itself.
- Scrum master
  He is responsible for adherence to the Scrum process and supports all project participants so that they can do their work.

4.8 Scrum Events

(a) What events are there in Scrum?
  - Sprint—this includes the other events
  - Sprint planning
  - Daily Scrum
  - Sprint review
  - Sprint retrospective

(b) Which of the events in Scrum are timeboxed and what are the guidelines?
  All events in Scrum follow the timebox principle. The following guidelines apply:
  - Sprint
    The duration of a sprint is defined by the Scrum team and may then neither be extended nor shortened. Two weeks are common.
  - Sprint planning
    2 h should be planned per sprint week.

- Daily Scrum
  The duration is set to 15 min.
- Sprint review
  1 h should be scheduled per sprint week.
- Sprint retrospective
  45 min. are recommended per sprint week.

4.9 Scrum Artifacts

Name the artifacts in Scrum.
- Product backlog
- Sprint backlog
- Increment

4.10 Merging

What strategies are there for integrating project results when project teams use both sequential and agile approaches within a project?

- Specification and development against interfaces
- Early integration with a minimal product

4.11 Acceptance

Where are the differences in project acceptance in the sequential and agile environment?
- Sequential:
  The acceptance is usually only complete at the end of the project. A check of the requirements implementation often provides extensive lists of deficiencies.
- Agile:

  Acceptances are made after each increment. Unfulfilled requirements can be taken into account in the next iteration in a timely manner.

Glossary[1]

Closure phase The last project phase brings together the final project activities.

Work package The smallest, indivisible element in the work breakdown structure, which can be located on any project structure level.

Task list Synonyms: *Action-Item-List* or *To-Do-List*.

Typical results of project meetings are information, results, decisions and tasks. Tasks should be stored in a task list, each task containing a description of the activities to be carried out, the respective responsible persons and the deadlines. A regular update of the task list shows a summary of the open points at the current time.

Effort estimation Estimation of the effort required to complete a work package (assuming 100% "pure project work").

Backlog Refinement Synonyms: *Backlog Grooming, Grooming, Product Backlog Refinement.*

Continuous process between the product owner and the development team to review and revise the entries in the product backlog.

Balanced Scorecard Concept for measuring, documenting and controlling the activities of a company or organization with respect to its vision and strategy. It usually includes a financial, customer, process and potential perspective.

Bar chart Synonym: bar diagram

Diagram for visualizing the time schedule of a project. The duration of a work package is represented by the length of a bar in the time axis. The bars can represent both actual and target data. Events correspond to points in time.

Best Practice Within a benchmarking process, the search is not for the theoretically or technically best option. Rather, the actual products or services offered in the market are compared with each other in terms of uniform quality criteria. The winner is then called "Best Practice".

---

[1]Note: The project management standards defined according to the DIN standards DIN 69901-5:2009 were taken from the project management glossary of the project magazine (Angermeier, Georg; URL: https://www.projektmagazin.de/glossarterm).

© Springer-Verlag GmbH Germany, part of Springer Nature 2022
D. Alam and U. Gühl, *Project Management for Practice,*
https://doi.org/10.1007/978-3-662-65159-9

BoM Bill of material

Burndown Chart Shows the current progress of work within a sprint and the remaining work still needed to achieve the sprint goal.

CCB Change Control Board

Coaching Generic term for different consulting methods. In the context of project management, a coach acts as an accompanying consultant who, by sharing his experience, supports the project manager.

COCOMO Constructive Cost Model
An algorithmic cost model used in software development for cost or effort estimation.

Controlling Processes and rules that contribute to securing the achievement of project objectives within project management.

CPPM Certified Professional for Project Management

Daily Scrum Event in Scrum for information exchange within the development team. Each team member explains his or her past and future activities in order to achieve the sprint goal. The scrum master is informed about obstacles.

Definition of Done Common understanding within a Scrum team of when a product backlog item or product increment is complete.

Definition of Ready Common understanding within a Scrum team of when a product backlog item is sufficiently articulated to be brought into a sprint backlog during a sprint planning.

Development Team Role in Scrum, responsible for implementing the sprint backlog and creating an increment. It is interdisciplinary and self-organized.

epic User story that is structured into further user stories.

GPM GPM German Association for Project Management e. V.

ICB IPMA Competence Baseline
International Project Management Standard and central reference of the GPM.

Increment Result of implementing the current sprint backlog.

IPMA International Project Management Association

IT Information Technology

KISS principle KISS stands for **K**eep **i**t **s**hort and **s**imple:[2] Use the simplest possible solutions.

Communication The exchange of information in order to share experiences or find solutions to problems between the project participants, in particular within the project team, is one of the key success factors of project management.

Communication plan A communication plan describes the communication, escalation and information channels in the project. It is the basis for the regulated and structured exchange of information within the project.

Cost schedule Representation of the costs expected to be incurred for the project. It is part of the project plan.

---

[2]There are also other meanings such as **K**eep **i**t **s**imple and **s**mart.

Creativity techniques Methods for stimulating creativity in developing new approaches to problem solving.

Crisis Unexpected difficult decision situation.

Critical path Within the network planning technique, the longest duration of the sequence of operations. If an operation is delayed on the critical path, the total project duration is extended.

CIP Continuous improvement process

Tender specification Synonyms: *Requirements catalog, requirements specification, rough concept, framework specification* or *system requirements.*

The set of requirements specified by the customer for the deliveries and services of a contractor within an order.

Magical triangle The magical triangle of project management means that the three central objectives of a project influence each other. These are, first, the quality requested forthe project goal; second, the time that might be spent on the project; and third, thecosts. If one objective changes, then one or both other objectives will change aswell.

Milestone Synonyms: *Release, Customer Release* or *Quality Gate.*

Event of special importance.

Method Method is the way to the goal. Method originally (Greek) means "path", i.e. by choosing a method, a way is sought to achieve a given goal.

Minimal Viable Product Firstusable version of a product produced with minimal effort. It should contain enough functionality that a customer or user can give feedback.

MTA Milestone Trend Analysis

MVP Minimal Viable Product

NCB National Competence Baseline

Network Technique Procedure for calculating the earliest possible starting timeand the latest necessary end time of the work packages.

Non-goal Non-goals are there to differentiate: they explicitly describe what shouldnot be reached in the project.

OEM Original Equipment Manufacturer

PDCA Plan, Do, Control, Act

Persona User models for the characterization of persons as representatives of user groups

Performance specification Synonyms: *Execution planning, detailed concept, functional specification, specification, project specification* or *actual concept.*

The performance specification includes the implementation plans developed by the contractor based on the tender specification handed over by the principal and thus concretizes the tender specification.

PgMP Program Management Professional

Planning Poker Estimation method for the implementation effort of a requirement.

Planning phase The planning phase includes planning activities and the definition of the project organization. This project phase is completed with the project plan and the kickoff meeting.

PM Project Management

PMBOK Project Management Body of Knowledge

PMBOK-Guide Guide to the Project Management Body of Knowledge

PMI Project Management Institute

PMO Project Management Office

PMP Project Management Professional

PRINCE2 Projects in Controlled Environments

Product Backlog Artifact in Scrum, contains prioritized requirements in the project.

Product Owner Role in Scrum, that is responsible for the requirements in the project, their content and prioritization, which are stored in the product backlog.

Projekt Intent, which is essentially characterized by uniqueness of the conditions in their totality.

Project Closure Formal end of a project.

Project order Synonyms: *Order, Project Manager Agreement* or *Project Agreement*. **Order to carry out a project.**

Project office Synonym: *Project Management Office (PMO)*.
The project office supports the project manager, but also project members mainly administratively, for example by creating and maintaining the project manual, organizing meetings, etc.

Project controlling Ensuring the achievement of all project goals.

Project documentation The totality of all relevant documents that arise in or from a project, are used or applied, or have other reference to the project.

Project manager Synonym: *Project* lead
The project manager is responsible to the principla for achieving the goals defined in the project order. For this purpose, she/he plans, controls and monitors the project.

Project Management Coordination of people and optimal use of resources to achieve project goals.

Project Organization Structural and procedural organization for the implementation of a specific project.

Project Phase Phase in the temporal course of the project, depending on the industry or type of project, caused by professional relationships.

Project Plan All plans present in the project.

Work Breakdown Structure A complete hierarchical representation of all elements (subprojects, work packages) of the project structure as a diagram or list. It is part of the project plan.

Project Goal The totality of individual goals to be achieved by the project.

Process A process has a defined beginning with an event or input. It describes a sequence of activities, optionally with intermediate results. There is a defined end with a result.

QM Quality Management

RACI Responsible (responsible for execution), Accountable (legally responsible), Consulted (advisory), Informed (will be informed)

Realization Phase This project phase includes all activities to achieve the defined project goals.

Requirements Engineering Requirements Engineering ensures that all requirements are known and documented in the project and that sufficient agreement of stakeholders is achieved with regard to these requirements.

Resource Within a project, resources include personnel and material resources used to complete the processes.

Resource Plan Synonyms: *Equipment Plan* or *Capacity Plan*.
Overview of the resources planned for one or more projects. It is part of the project plan.

Risk Management Elimination, avoidance or reduction of project risks.

ROI Return on Investment

RUP Rational Unified Process

Scope Management Synonym: *Content and scope management*.
Scope Management ensures that, based on the project goals, the project scope is defined, developed and its implementation is ensured. All corresponding work tasks are usually stored in the work breakdown structure.

Scrum Master Role in Scrum, is responsible for the processes in the Scrum project. He is also responsible for ensuring that the development team can work well by, for example, removing obstacles.

Soft skills Synonyms: *Social competence, soft factors*.
Cross-professional skills for dealing with oneself and others, which supplement the professional skills and qualifications.

Sprint Central part of Scrum with a fixed time period, typically two weeks. A sprint is a container for events in Scrum. The goal of a sprint is to create an increment in the form of usable software.

Sprint Backlog Artifact in Scrum, contains the part of the product backlog to be implemented in a sprint.

Sprint Planning Event in Scrum to determine the sprint backlog.

Sprint Retrospective Event in Scrum, reflection of the development team for continuous process improvement.

Sprint Review Event in Scrum, highlight at the end of a sprint for the Scrum team and stakeholders. The development team presents the increment with the implemented sprint backlog to the product owner and stakeholders.

Stakeholder All those who can influence the project, are interested in the project or are affected by the project.

Steering Committee Synonyms: *Decision-making Committee, Management Committee, Project Committee* or *Review Board*.

The steering commtitteeis the supervisory body of the project. Members of the steering committee are the principal, typically as chairman, as well as the key stakeholders from the internal organization.

Strategy Phase The basic, first project phase typically includes analyses, clarification of the task and ends with a project order.

Stretched Objective Entry in the sprint backlog, which is not relevant for the sprint goal.

Task Board A task board reflects the current state of work in the sprint. It contains the sprint backlog entries to be implemented as well as the associated tasks. Based on the position in the task board, the work status of the tasks and thus the implementation status of the associated sprint backlog entries is visible.

Time schedule Synonym: *Timetable*.

Graphicrepresentation of the duration of the individual work packages within a project, for example in the form of bar or network diagrams. It is part of the project plan.

Trend Analysis In the project management environment, this is a mathematical technique that uses historical results to predict future results. Variations in costs and operational procedures are recorded.

User Story Short description of a requirement with the motivation of a role

WBS Work Breakdown Structure

WP Work package

Work in Progress In Kanban, tasks are assigned to columns in a Kanban board. Each column represents a process activity. The number of tasks in a column then represents "work in progress". The goal is to limit the tasks within a column, expressed as *work in progress limit*.

Goal definition Quantitative and qualitative definition of the project content and the conditions to be met for implementation.

Index

© Springer-Verlag GmbH Germany, part of Springer Nature 2022
D. Alam and U. Gühl, *Project Management for Practice*,
https://doi.org/10.1007/978-3-662-65159-9

Printed in the United States
by Baker & Taylor Publisher Services